The Battle of Gettysburg As Seen by Two Teens: The Stories of Tillie Pierce and Daniel Skelly

Edited by Frank Meredith

Introduction by Dianne E. Dusman

SAVANNAH BOOKS

Cover art, *The Battle of Gettysburg, PA, July 3rd, 1863* by Currier and Ives (Library of Congress)

Rear cover photograph of Tillie Pierce courtesy of Keith Grandstaff

Text and illustrations in Matilda Pierce Alleman's *At Gettysburg: What a Girl Saw and Heard of the Battle* courtesy of Keith Grandstaff

Text and photographs in Daniel Skelly's *A Boy's Experiences During the Battles of Gettysburg* courtesy of John Heiser of the Gettysburg National Military Park

Layout and design: Frank Meredith

Order this book online at www.TheUnfinishedWork.com

Published by Savannah Books, Inc., 146 Grand St., Schoharie, NY 12157

ISBN: 1449900895

EAN-13: 978-1449900892

TABLE OF CONTENTS

FOREWORD

What an exciting time to be a Civil War buff! With the 150th anniversaries of the war taking place in the years 2011-2015, there will be a great number of special events, reenactments, and commemorations, giving tens of thousands of reenactors (both military *and* civilian) the opportunity to share their carefully researched and prepared "living history" interpretations.

Without doubt, the pre-eminent activities will take place in Gettysburg, PA—and rightfully so, because it was in this crossroads town of 2,600 residents in July 1863 that the Union Army narrowly avoided a crushing defeat, at a time when such a loss might well have brought an end to the war, thus allowing the Confederate States of America to stand as a separate, sovereign nation. (If that had happened, how long would it have been before the two countries were once again at war?)

Many "what ifs" surround this crucial battle. Hundreds of books about Gettysburg have been written and hundreds more will follow, but few can match the poignancy and behind-the-scenes immediacy found in the eyewitness accounts of teenagers Tillie Pierce and Daniel Skelly.

One cannot help but admire the courage, spunk, and feistiness displayed by Tillie in the face of scenes no young woman should ever have to experience. Her compassion and care for the wounded are shining examples of the way so many women on both sides of the battle lines worked tirelessly to aide the suffering—and in many cases, horribly disfigured—men. Tillie's words reveal a great deal about her character, and her story includes many fascinating anecdotes and details that would otherwise have been lost to history. It is no wonder this heroine's book remains in print after all these years; and her childhood home on Baltimore Street has been painstakingly and lovingly restored by Keith and Leslie Grandstaff as *The Tillie Pierce House Bed and Breakfast*.

While the war caught up with Tillie in the midst of a typical school day, young store clerk Daniel Skelly had already begun what would become a lifelong career in business. Away from Gettysburg when the Confederate invasion of Pennsylvania began, he hurried back home in time to experience two days of waiting and wondering as General Lee's Army drew nearer and nearer, their evening campfires visible in the distance. He witnessed the Union Army's retreat through town and described what many of the townsfolk experienced during the three days of battle—and its horrific aftermath. His venture selling tobacco to some of the Union soldiers reveals his entrepreneurial spirit, though some people might choose to view it as war profiteering. Daniel closes his story with his account of President Abraham Lincoln's visit to Gettysburg four months later for the dedication of the new National cemetery: the final place of rest for many of the 7,800 men who sacrificed their lives during this turning point in American history.

Today, we in America can scarcely imagine what it is like to experience the horrors of war in our own countryside, let alone in our streets and yards. As a nine-year-old boy in 1963, I witnessed the 100th Anniversary reenactment of the Battle of Hanover, PA—the first battle on Union soil, occurring the day before the Battle of Gettysburg began. Forty-seven years later, I vividly recall the sights and smells and sounds of hundreds of cavalrymen galloping through the center of my hometown, their gunfire echoing like booming cannon shots in the confined space, their horses straining amidst the turmoil and terrifying conditions of "war," the "wounded" and "dying" soldiers in the street . . . and that was merely a reenactment. I can scarcely imagine the impact on me if those events really happened.

But that is the point of any reenactment. It is far more significant than men and women dressing up to play soldier for a day. Such things really *did* happen. Men suffered and died. Women ignored their inner trepidations and tended the wounded and dying men. Why?

Of the various reasons men fought in the Civil War and women rushed to aid the fallen, I believe the most compelling motivation is summed up in the word *duty*. As the revered Gen. Robert E. Lee once said, "Do your duty in all things. You cannot do more; you should never wish to do less."

I fear that in America today, too many of us have lost sight of the significance of the word duty and its place in building our character. Unfortunately, we seem to live in a culture that prefers to let someone else do our "dirty work" for us. It is my hope that as we read the inspiring stories of Tillie Pierce and Daniel Skelly, we will each feel the desire to answer the call to fulfill our duty to help make our communities and country the finest they can be.

NOTE ON PUNCTUATION

The rules of punctuation, capitalization, and spelling have changed since Tillie and Daniel wrote their stories. I have resisted the temptation to edit their work to conform to modern usage. Perhaps English teachers may wish to use some excerpts for "correction" in their classroom?

INTRODUCTION

The Spirit of Tillie Pierce

As a fifteen-year-old girl growing up in Hanover, Pennsylvania (only a few miles from Gettysburg) over one hundred years after the battle, the thought of war in my own back yard never entered my mind. In fact, I grew to adulthood in my little town without ever observing even the smallest act of violence against another human being.

Against the backdrop of my own life, the articulate accounts of fifteen-year-old Tillie Pierce's memories of the Battle of Gettysburg are, at times, chilling and at other times comforting. We see in her uncommon courage and strength during the events leading up to the battle and while dealing with its grotesque aftermath.

The thread throughout her account, though, is her unwavering willingness to help—to feed the hungry, to give water to the thirsty, to bandage the wounded, even to comfort the dying. As I read her account, I asked myself whether civilians today in our country would be so willing as Tillie was to do such things? Or would doors and windows slam shut in the face of devastation, death and despair, without knowing whether friend or foe was knocking?

My hope is that the spark of Tillie's spirit may live on in men and women in every place where unexpected violence and adversity rain down—and that, as we read her account of the events at Gettysburg, we remember the women, men, and children throughout the world who experience acts of violence every day of their lives and hope for women like Tillie Pierce to appear.

Dianne E. Dusman
Wellsville, PA
May 6, 2010

PHOTOGRAPHS, MAPS, AND ILLUSTRATIONS

(DS) – **Daniel Skelly's book**
(GD) – **GettysburgDaily.com**
(HJ) – **Map by Hal Jespersen, www.posix.com/CW**
(KG) – **Keith Grandstaff**
(LC) – **Library of Congress**
(MA) – **Matilda Pierce Alleman's book**
(NA) – **National Archives**
(SI) – **Smithsonian Institution**

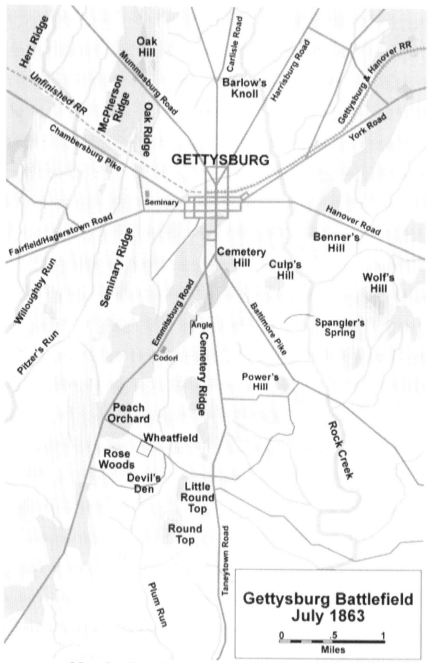

Map by Hal Jespersen, www.posix.com/CW
See six more of Mr. Jesperson's maps,
beginning on page 104.

SETTING THE SCENE

As the Confederate States of America's "Second War of Independence" entered its third year in June of 1863, Gen. Robert E. Lee decided to launch a major assault on Northern territory. His native Virginia had suffered mightily after two summers of battles and foraging by both armies, so it was high time the Yankee farmers bore their share of lost crops, livestock, and farmlands. Besides, the political pressure continued to mount on President Abraham Lincoln, especially since his Emancipation Proclamation had gone into effect on the first of the year. Few men on either side of the conflict would have given "slavery" as the primary reason for risking their lives. Lee was convinced that if his army could win a major battle on Northern soil—perhaps capture a major city such as Harrisburg and threaten Philadelphia and New York—then Lincoln would have no choice but to end the war and allow the Confederacy to stand as the free and sovereign nation they believed themselves to be.

By mid-June, rumors of the Confederate invasion set southern Pennsylvania into a state of panic. Since there were no regular Union Army units within range to intervene, Governor Curtain called for volunteers to form emergency militia units, and he ordered the evacuation of livestock and valuables to points east of the Susquehanna River. Freed African-Americans were particularly distressed, fearful of being captured by Rebels as "contraband" (escaped slaves) and sent South into servitude. The small crossroads town of Gettysburg included more than 180 African-Americans amongst its 2,600 citizens. With the abundance of roads that converged on the town (see map opposite), it seemed likely that it was only a matter of time before the Confederate Army paid a visit. By the last week of June, most of the African-Americans had fled Gettysburg, never to return.

Emergency Militia units patrolled points west, and they had already had several encounters with Rebel scouts and foragers. On June 21st, a daring assault by forty volunteer cavalrymen drove 160 veteran Confederate cavalry back into the mountains several miles west of town. But Lee's Army was closing in. On the morning of June 26th, 700 Emergency Militia recruits (with only two days of training!) arrived in Gettysburg. Two hours later, they were on the march to stand in the way of Lee's advance. . . .

THE NATIONAL MONUMENT AT GETTYSBURG

AT GETTYSBURG

OR

What a Girl Saw and Heard of the Battle.

A TRUE NARRATIVE.

BY

MRS. TILLIE (PIERCE) ALLEMAN.

NEW YORK,
W. LAKE BORLAND,
1889.

CONTENTS

ILLUSTRATIONS

PREFACE

The experience of a little girl during three days of a hard fought battle, as portrayed in this volume, is certainly of rare occurrence and very likely has never been realized before. Such a narrative as the following is worthy of preservation among the pages of our nations literature. The story is told with such marked faithfulness, such honesty of expression, such vividness of portrayal, that those who lived in and passed through those scenes, or similar ones, will at once recognize the situations and surroundings as natural and real.

While perusing its pages, the veteran will again live in the days gone by; when he tramped the dusty march, joined in the terrible charge, or suffered in the army hospital. The Heroine of this book performed her part well; but it is doubtful whether, at the time, she fully realized the heart-felt thanks and noble thoughts that sprang from the "Boys in Blue" in response to her heroism and kindness.

How vividly is presented the weary march to the field of conflict; our eagerness to quaff the sparkling water as she handed it to us, fresh from the cooling spring. We thanked her, but she did not hear the full gratitude that was in our hearts.

Who but a soldier can know the welling emotions in that dying general's breast, when, perhaps for the first time in many months, he gazed into an innocent and child-like face, seeing naught but tender love and deep sympathy. Did she not, in part, take the place of those near and dear to his heart, but who, on that fearful night were many miles away? How his thoughts must have flashed homeward!

And oh! the tender chords that must have been touched in his valiant soul! No wonder he looked "so earnestly" in her face. He was feasting on the sympathies that sprang from her heart and illumined her countenance. She did greater things than she knew, and her reward will follow. But we shall refer to no more scenes. They are many and varied. In their contemplation, the reader will experience his own thoughts and emotions.

We have been asked to write a preface to her narrative; but we cannot slight this opportunity of thanking her in the name of the "Boys in Blue," and all patriots, for what she did.

We are truly glad to have this touching and thrilling story of her experience at the battle of Gettysburg, even though after many years; and our only regret is that many of our comrades have answered to the last roll-call before its publication.

We will rejoice in its publication, and wide circulation; for it is deserving a welcome, not only in public libraries, but in the family circle of every American. It cannot fail to interest and instruct both old and young. The book will speak for itself.

A VETERAN.

Matilda "Tillie" Pierce

CHAPTER I

INTRODUCTION

Impressed with the fact that incidents connected with the Battle of Gettysburg are daily becoming more appreciated, and believing that the recital of those occurrences will awaken new interest as time rolls on, I am constrained to transmit in some tangible form my knowledge of the place now so historic, as well as my experience during those thrilling days of July, 1863. Nor is it with any desire to be classed among the heroines of that period, that these lines are written; but simply to show what many a patriotic and loyal girl would have done if surrounded by similar circumstances.

In truth, the history of those days contains numerous instances in which America's daughters, loyal to their country and flag, have experienced, suffered, and sacrificed far more than did the present writer. In their behalf, and as a legacy to my own offspring, I therefore pen these lines and deem it unnecessary to make any further apology.

Gettysburg is my native place. As is doubtless known to many of my readers, it is most pleasantly located in a healthful region of country, near the southern border of Pennsylvania. Prior to the battle it was comparatively unknown to the outside world, save to those interested in the Lutheran College and Theological Seminary here located. From year to year, it pursued the even and quiet tenor of an inland town, with nothing to vary the monotony but the annual exercises of the above-named institutions. On these occasions, the influx of strangers for the short period of commencement week did add some stir and life to the place, but only to have it settle into more irksome quietude after the visitors and their dear boys had left.

Today, Gettysburg is a changed place. A new spirit and enterprise have taken hold of its inhabitants, and evidences of improvement and modern progress are everywhere manifest. Scarcely a day passes that does not witness some pilgrimage to this Mecca of loyal devotion to human freedom.

It is almost needless to state that I am still strongly attached to the place, its surroundings and associations, though for many years my home has been in another part of the State. Fondly do I cherish the scenes of my childhood. Often do I think of the lovely groves on and around Culp's Hill; of the mighty boulders which there abound, upon which we often spread the picnic feast; of the now famous Spangler's Spring, where we drank the cooling draught on those peaceful summer days. There too, our merry peals of laughter mingled with the sweet warbling of the birds. What pleasant times were ours as we went berrying along the quiet, sodded lane that leads from the town to that now memorable hill.

From my mind can never be effaced those far off mountains to the west, whose distant horizon gave a gorgeousness to sunsets, which, when once seen, can never be forgotten. Beholding those various tinted ephemeral isles, in that sea of occidental glory, one could not help thinking of the possibilities of the grandeur in the beyond. The effect could be none other than transporting.

As I often stood in the quiet Evergreen Cemetery, when we knew naught but the smiles of Peace, gazing to the distant South Mountains, or the nearer Round Tops, or Culp's Hill, little did I dream that from those summits the engines of war would, in a few years, belch forth their missiles of destruction; that through those sylvan aisles would reverberate the clash of arms, the roar of musketry, and the booming of cannon, to be followed by the groans of the wounded and dying.

Little did I think that those lovely valleys, teeming with verdure and the rich harvest, would soon be strewn with the distorted and mangled bodies of American brothers; making a rich ingathering for the grim monster, Death; that across that peaceful lane would charge the brave and daring "Louisiana Tigers," thirsting for their brother's blood, but soon to be hurled back, filling the space over which they advanced with their shattered and dead bodies.

Such is the transition which in my girlhood days I was made to realize. The horrors of war are fully known only to those who have seen and heard them. It was my lot to see and hear only part, but it was sufficient.

To-day, many of my dear, former associates of Gettysburg are gone. The kind and sweet faces of the old fathers and mothers have passed beyond the veil. They whom I used to love and honor now sleep their last sleep beneath the sods of that memorable valley. No more will they narrate their experiences of that terrible conflict; nor tell how they cared for and sheltered the wounded; the narrow escapes they made from stray shots; their property taken or destroyed.

With pleasant recollections I bring to mind the Young Ladies' Seminary on the corner of High and Washington Streets. Here I received instruction; here, in the bright and happy flush of young womanhood, I was graduated and given my diploma.

Within those same walls had been placed some of the wounded and dying heroes of the struggle; and as we passed from room to room we would speak in subdued tones of the solemn scenes which imagination and report placed before our minds as having transpired when the conflict was over.

The old College Church on Chambersburg Street, once a battle hospital, afterwards witnessed the ceremony that made me a happy bride. The very streets, the homes, the sanctuaries, even the tones of their bells, the hour's stroke of the Court House clock. the familiar faces and voices of the citizens at the period of which I now write, all cling to my recollection and are endeared to my heart, as only the memories of childhood and youth can endear.

My native townsmen, during that terrible struggle, acted as patriotic and bravely as it was possible for citizens to act, who had suddenly thrust upon them the most gigantic battle of modern times. They had none of the weapons or munitions of war; they were not drilled and were totally unprepared for such an unthought of experience. They were civilians. Long before had many of their sons and brothers gone to the front, and those who still remained were as true to the Union as those found at home in the other towns of the North.

Upon the first rumor of the rebel invasion, Major Robert Bell, a citizen of the place, recruited a company of cavalry from the town and surrounding country. A company of infantry was also formed from the students and citizens of the place, which was mustered into Col. Wm. Jennings' regiment of

Pennsylvania Emergency Troops. This regiment, on June 26th, was the first to encounter and exchange shots with the invaders of 1863. Though inexperienced, the stand they made, and the valor they displayed before an overwhelming force, cannot fail in placing the loyalty and bravery of her citizens in the foremost rank.

Opportunity was offered a few, who like old John Burns, went into the fray. To some, like Professors Jacobs and Stower, came the occasion of explaining and pointing out to the Union officers the impregnable positions of the locality, and by this means insuring victory to our arms. To others was given the opportunity of concealing in their homes the brave Union boys who had been wounded in the first day's fight, who, in their retreat, had sought shelter in the house they could first reach, and there were compelled to remain, within the Confederate lines, during the remainder of the battle. Many a Union soldier would have gone to "Libby" or "Andersonville" had it not been for the loyalty and bravery of some of the citizens in thus secreting them.

To all was presented the opportunity of caring for the wounded and dying after the battle had passed, and nobly and feebly did they administer the tender and loving acts of charity even in their own homes, as well as upon the field and in the hospital. Let those disposed to cavil and doubt the patriotism of the citizens of Gettysburg at the time of the battle forever cease, for what I have written is correct. True it is there were a few who sympathized with the South, just as in other Northern towns, but it would be unjust and unreasonable to condemn the many for the misdeeds of the few.

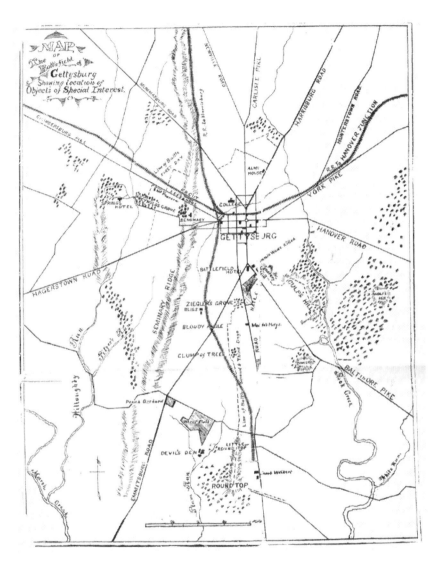

MAP OF THE BATTLEFIELD OF GETTYSBURG

CHAPTER II

INCIDENTS PRECEDING THE BATTLE

Before entering into a description of what I saw during the battle, it may be interesting to narrate some of the preceding events that occurred. We had often heard that the rebels were about to make a raid, but had always found it a false alarm. An amusing incident connected with these reported raids was the manner in which some of our older men prepared to meet the foe.

I remember one evening in particular, when quite a number of them had assembled to guard the town that night against an attack from the enemy. They were "armed to the teeth" with old, rusty guns and swords, pitchforks, shovels and pick-axes. Their falling into line, the manœuvers, the commands given and not heeded, would have done a veteran's heart good. I have often sat and listened to these well-meaning citizens laugh over the contemplation of their comical aspect.

On these occasions it was also amusing to behold the conduct of the colored people of the town. Gettysburg had a goodly number of them. They regarded the Rebels as having an especial hatred toward them, and believed that if they fell into their hands, annihilation was sure. These folks mostly lived in the southwestern part of the town, and their flight was invariably down Breckenridge Street and Baltimore Street, and toward the woods on and around Culp's Hill.

I can see them yet; men and women with bundles as large as old-fashioned feather ticks slung across their backs, almost bearing them to the ground. Children also, carrying their bundles and striving in vain to keep up with their seniors. The greatest consternation was depicted on all their countenances as they hurried along; crowding and running against each other in their confusion; children stumbling, falling, and crying. Mothers, anxious for their offspring, would stop for a moment to hurry them up, saying: "*Fo' de Lod's sake, you chillen, cum right long quick! If dem Rebs dun kotch you, dey tear you all up;*" and similar expressions. These terrible warnings were sure to have the desired effect; for, with their eyes open wider than ever, they were not long in hastening their steps.

About three weeks before the battle, rumors were again rife of the coming of the rebel horde into our own fair and prosperous State. This caused the greatest alarm; and our hearts often throbbed with fear and trembling. To many of us, such a visit meant destruction of home, property and perhaps life.

We were informed they had crossed the State line, then were at Chambersburg, then at Carlisle, then at or near Harrisburg, and would soon have possession of our capital. We had often heard of their taking horses and cattle, carrying off property and destroying buildings. A week had hardly elapsed when another alarm beset us. "The Rebels are coming! The Rebels are coming!" was passed from lip to lip, and all was again consternation.

We were having our regular literary exercises on Friday afternoon, at our Seminary, when the cry reached our ears. Rushing to the door and standing on the front portico, we beheld in the direction of the Theological Seminary a dark, dense mass, moving toward town. Our teacher, Mrs. Eyster, at once said: "Children, run home as quickly as you can." It did not require repeating. I am satisfied some of the girls did not reach their homes before the Rebels were in the streets.

As for myself, I had scarcely reached the front door when, on looking up the street, I saw some of the men on horseback. I scrambled in, slammed shut the door, and hastening to the sitting room, peeped out between the shutters.

What a horrible sight! There they were, human beings! Clad almost in rags, covered with dust, riding wildly, pell-mell down the hill toward our home! Shouting, yelling most unearthly, cursing, brandishing their revolvers, and firing right and left. I was fully persuaded that the Rebels had actually come at last. What they would do with us was a fearful question to my young mind.

Soon the town was filled with infantry, and then the searching and ransacking began in earnest. They wanted horses, clothing, anything and almost everything they could conveniently carry away. Nor were they particular about asking. Whatever suited them they took. They did, however, make a formal demand of the town authorities for a large supply of flour, meat, groceries, shoes, hats, and (doubtless, not least in their estimations), ten barrels of whiskey; or, in lieu of all this, five thousand dollars. But our merchants and bankers had too often heard of their coming and had already shipped their wealth to places of safety. Thus it was that a few days after, the citizens of York were compelled to make up our proportion of the Rebel requisition.

I have often thought what a laughable spectacle this wing of Southern chivalry would have presented on dress parade, had they obtained and donned the variety of hats generally found upon the shelves of a village store. But they were reduced to extremity and doubtless were not particular.

Upon the report of, and just previous to this raid, the citizens had sent their horses out the Baltimore Pike, as far as the Cemetery. There they were to be kept until those having the care of them were signaled that the enemy was about, when they were to hasten as fast as possible in the direction of Baltimore. Along with this party, Father sent our own horse in charge of the hired boy we then had living with us. I was very much attached to the animal, for she was gentle and very pretty. I had often ridden her. The cavalry, referred to above, came so suddenly that no signal was given. They overtook the boys with the horses, captured, and brought them all back to town.

As they were passing our house, my mother beckoned to the raiders, and some of them rode over to where she was standing and asked what was the matter, Mother said to them: "You don't want the boy! He is not our boy, he is only living with us."

One of the men replied: "No, we don't want the boy, you can have him; we are only after the horses."

About this time the boy's sister, who was standing a short distance off, screamed at the top of her voice to Mother: "If the Rebs take our Sam, I don't know what I'll do with you folks!" Thus, holding us responsible for her brother Sam's safety even in times like that.

Mother, however, assured her that they were after horses and not their Sam.

After we saw that the boy was safe, Mother and I began to plead for the horse. As I stood there begging and weeping, I was so shocked and insulted I shall never forget it.

One impudent and coarse Confederate said to me: "Sissy, what are you crying about? Go in the house and mind your business."

I felt so indignant at his treatment, I only wished I could have had some manner of revenge on the fellow. They left, however, without giving us any satisfaction.

About one-half hour after this, some of these same raiders came back and, stopping at the kitchen door, asked Mother for something to eat. She replied: "Yes, you ought to come back and ask for something to eat after taking a person's horse." She nevertheless gave them some food, for Mother always had a kind and noble heart, even toward her enemies.

Their manner of eating was shocking in the extreme. As I stood in a doorway and saw them laughing and joking at their deeds of the day, they threw the apple butter in all directions while spreading their bread. I was heartily glad when they left, for they were a rude set.

While they were still in the kitchen, my mother pleaded earnestly for our horse, so they told her that if we would go to Colonel White, then commander, we might, perhaps, get the horse back. Father went with them; but when he got before Colonel White, he was informed by that officer that he understood father was "A black Abolitionist; so black, that he was turning black;" also, that he understood that he had two sons in the Union Army, whom he supposed had taken as much from the South as they were now taking from him. So my father returned without the horse.

This information given to the Rebels, we afterwards learned, was the act of Sam's sister, referred to above. I am afraid her sympathies were not as much for the Union as they should have been. She certainly manifested a very unkind disposition toward our family, who had been doing all we could for her brother. It would surprise a great many to learn who this person was, but as no detraction is intended, I will dismiss the subject at once.

We frequently saw the Rebels riding our horse up and down the street, until at last she became so lame she could hardly get along. That was the last we saw of her, and I felt that I had been robbed of a dear friend.

While the infantry were moving about the town in squads searching for booty, and while we were all standing at the front door looking at their movements and wondering what they would do next, I remember that my mother, not noticing any in the immediate vicinity, spoke to a neighbor on the opposite side of the street saying: "What a filthy, dirty looking set! One cannot tell them from the street."

Father said: "You had better be careful; there is one of them at the curb-stone right in front of us, tying his shoe."

Mother exclaimed: "Oh my! I didn't see him!"

They were actually so much the color of the street, that it was no wonder we failed to notice this one.

That evening, when these raiders were leaving, they ran all the cars that were about out to the railroad bridge east of the town, set the bridge and cars on fire, and destroyed the track. We were informed that they had gone to York, a thriving town about twenty-five miles to the northeast.

A little before noon on Tuesday, June 30th, a great number of Union cavalry began to arrive in the town. They passed northwardly along Washington Street, turned toward the west on reaching Chambersburg Street, and passed out in the direction of the Theological Seminary. It was to me a novel and grand sight. I had never seen so many soldiers at one time. They were Union soldiers and that was enough for me, for I then knew we had protection, and I felt they were our dearest friends. I afterwards learned that these men were Buford's cavalry, numbering about six thousand men.

A crowd of "us girls" were standing on the corner of Washington and High Streets as these soldiers passed by. Desiring to encourage them, who, as we were told, would before long be in battle, my sister started to sing the old war song "Our Union Forever." As some of us did not know the whole of the piece we kept repeating the chorus. Thus we sought to cheer our brave men; and we felt amply repaid when we saw that our efforts were appreciated. Their countenances brightened and we received their thanks and cheers. After the battle, some of these soldiers told us that the singing was very good, but that they would have liked to have heard more than the chorus.

The movements of this day, in addition to what we beheld a few days previous, told plainly that some great military event was coming pretty close to us. The town was all astir and every one was anxious. Thus, in the midst of great excitement and solicitude, the day passed. As we lay down for the night, little did we think what the morrow would bring forth.

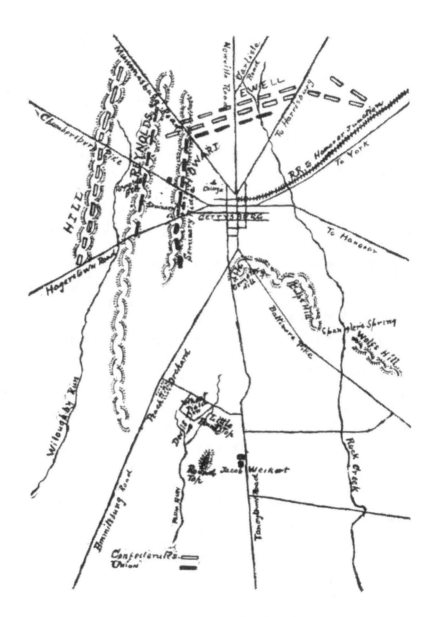

MAP OF THE FIRST DAY'S BATTLE

CHAPTER III

DURING THE FIRST DAY OF THE BATTLE

We awoke early. It was impossible to become drowsy with the events of the previous day uppermost in our minds. We were prompt enough at breakfast that morning.

As more soldiers were expected, and in order to show how welcome they would be, my sister and I had, on the previous evening, prepared a tableful of boquets which we intended to hand or throw to them as they passed our house.

We had no sooner finished our breakfast when it was announced that troops were coming. We hastened up what we called the side street, (Breckenridge,) and on reaching Washington Street, again saw some of our army passing.

First came a long line of cavalry, then wagon after wagon passed by for quite awhile. Again we sang patriotic songs as they moved along. Some of these wagons were filled with stretchers and other articles; in others we noticed soldiers reclining, who were doubtless in some way disabled.

It was between nine and ten o'clock when we first noticed firing in the direction of Seminary Ridge. At first the sound was faint, then it grew louder. Soon the booming of cannon was heard, then great clouds of smoke were seen rising beyond the ridge. The sound became louder and louder, and was now incessant. The troops passing us moved faster, the men had now become excited and urged on their horses. The battle was waging. This was my first terrible experience.

I remember hearing some of the soldiers remarking that there was no telling how soon some of them would be brought back in those ambulances, or carried on the stretchers. I hardly knew what it meant, but I learned afterward, even before the day had passed.

It was almost noon when the last of the train had passed and I began to think of dinner and the folks at home. I hurried back, and the first thing that met my gaze as I passed the parlor was the table full of flowers. The soldiers had passed and we had not given them the boquets. They did not come by our house and in our haste to see them, we had forgotten all about the intended welcome.

Entering the dining-room I found dinner waiting, but I was too excited to eat, and so, soon finished my meal. After I had eaten what that day I called dinner, our neighbor, Mrs. Schriver, called at the house and said she would leave the town and go to her father's (Jacob Weikert), who lived on the Taneytown road at the eastern slope of the Round Top.

Mr. Schriver, her husband, was then serving in the Union army, so that under all the circumstances at this time surrounding her, Mrs. Schriver did not feel safe in the house.

As the battle had commenced and was still progressing at the west of the town, and was not very far off, she thought it safer for herself and two children to go to her parents, who lived about three miles to the south. She requested that I be permitted to accompany her, and as it was regarded a safer place for me than to remain in town, my parents readily consented that I should go.

The only preparation I made for the departure was to carry my best clothes down to the cellar, so that they might be safe when I returned; never thinking of taking any along, nor how long I would stay.

FLEEING FROM DANGER

About one o'clock we started on foot; the battle still going on. We proceeded out Baltimore Street and entered the Evergreen Cemetery. This was our easiest and most direct route, as it would bring us to the Taneytown road a little further on.

As we were passing along the Cemetery hill, our men were already planting cannon. They told us to hurry as fast as possible; that we were in great danger of being shot by the Rebels, whom they expected would shell toward us at any moment. We fairly ran to get out of this new danger.

As I looked toward the Seminary Ridge I could see and hear the confusion of the battle. Troops moving hither and thither; the smoke of the conflict arising from the fields; shells bursting in the air, together with the din, rising and falling in mighty undulations. These things, beheld for the first time, filled my soul with the greatest apprehensions.

We soon reached the Taneytown road, and while traveling along, were overtaken by an ambulance wagon in which was the body of a dead soldier. Some of the men told us that it was the body of General Reynolds, and that he had been killed during the forenoon in the battle.

We continued on our way, and had gotten to a little one and a half story house, standing on the west side of the road, when, on account of the muddy condition of the road, we were compelled to stop. This place on the following day became General Meade's headquarters.

Meade's Headquarters (LC)

While we were standing at the gate, not knowing what to do or where to go, a soldier came out and kindly told us he would try to get some way to help us further on, as it was very dangerous to remain there.

It began to look as though we were getting into new dangers at every step, instead of getting away from them.

We went into the house and after waiting a short time, this same soldier came to us saying: "Now I have a chance for you. There is a wagon coming down the road and I will try to get them to make room for you."

The wagon was already quite full, but the soldier insisted and prevailed. We fully appreciated his kindness, and as he helped us on the wagon we thanked him very much.

But what a ride! I shall never forget it. The mud was almost up to the hubs of the wheels, and underneath the mud were rocks. The wagon had no springs, and as the driver was anxious to put the greatest distance between himself and the battle in the least time possible, the jolting and bumping were brought out to perfection. At last we reached Mr. Weikert's and were gladly welcomed to their home.

It was not long after our arrival, until Union artillery came hurrying by. It was indeed a thrilling sight. How the men impelled heir horses! How the officers urged the men as they all flew past toward the sound of the battle! Now the road is getting all cut up; they take to the fields, and all is an anxious, eager hurry! Shouting, lashing the horses, cheering the men, they all rush madly on.

Suddenly we behold an explosion; it is that of a caisson. We see a man thrown high in the air and come down in a wheat field close by. He is picked up and carried into the house. As they pass by I see his eyes are blown out and his whole person seems to be one black mass. The first words I hear him say is: "Oh dear! I forgot to read my Bible to-day! What will my poor wife and children say?"

I saw the soldiers carry him up stairs; they laid him upon a bed and wrapped him in cotton. How I pitied that poor man! How terribly the scenes of war were being irresistibly portrayed before my vision.

After the artillery had passed, infantry began coming. I soon saw that these men were very thirsty and would go to the spring which is on the north side of the house.

I was not long in learning what I could do. Obtaining a bucket, I hastened to the spring, and there, with others, carried water to the moving column until the spring was empty. We then went to the pump standing on the south side of the house, and supplied water from it. Thus we continued giving water to our tired soldiers until night came on, when we sought rest indoors.

It was toward the close of the afternoon of this day that some of the wounded from the field of battle began to arrive where I was staying. They reported hard fighting, many wounded and killed, and were afraid our troops would be defeated and perhaps routed.

The first wounded soldier whom I met had his thumb tied up. This I thought was dreadful, and told him so.

"Oh," said he, "this is nothing; you'll see worse than this before long."

"Oh! I hope not," I innocently replied.

Soon two officers carrying their arms in slings made their appearance, and I more fully began to realize that something terrible had taken place.

Now the wounded began to come in greater numbers. Some limping, some with their heads and arms in bandages, some crawling, others carried on stretchers or brought in ambulances. Suffering, cast down and dejected, it was a truly pitiable gathering. Before night the barn was filled with the shattered and dying heroes of this day's struggle.

That evening Beckie Weikert, the daughter at home, and I went out to the barn to see what was transpiring there. Nothing before in my experience had ever paralleled the sight we then and there beheld. There were the groaning and crying, the struggling and dying, crowded side by side, while attendants sought to aid and relieve them as best they could. We were so overcome by the sad and awful spectacle that we hastened back to the house weeping bitterly.

As we entered the basement or cellar-kitchen of the house, we found many nurses making beef tea for the wounded. Seeing that we were crying they inquired as to the cause. We told them where we had been and what we had seen. They no doubt appreciated our feelings for they at once endeavored to cheer us by telling funny stories, and ridiculing our tears. They soon dispelled our terror and caused us to laugh so much that many times when we should have been sober minded we were not; the reaction having been too sudden for our overstrung nerves.

I remember that at this time a chaplain who was present in the kitchen stepped up to me while I was attending to some duty and said: "Little girl, do all you can for the poor soldiers and the Lord will reward you."

I looked up in his face and laughed, but at once felt ashamed of my conduct and begged his pardon. After telling him what Beckie and I had seen, how the nurses had derided us for crying and that I now laughed when I should not, being unable to help myself, he remarked: "Well it is much better for you and the soldiers to be in a cheerful mood."

The first day had passed, and with the rest of the family, I retired, surrounded with strange and appalling events, and many new visions passing rapidly through my mind.

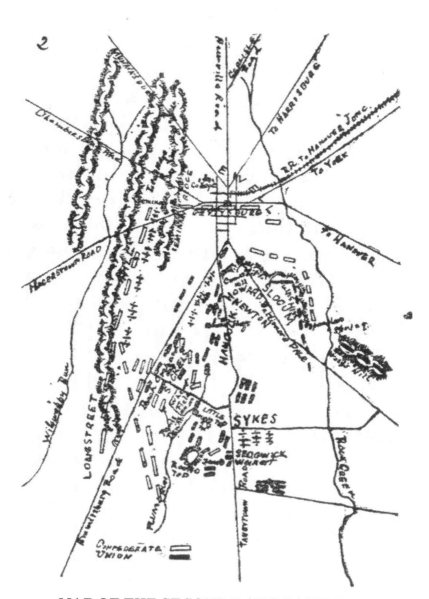

MAP OF THE SECOND DAY'S BATTLE

CHAPTER IV

DURING THE SECOND DAY OF THE BATTLE

The day dawned bright and clear; the hot rays of the July sun soon fell upon the landscape. As quickly as possible I hurried out of the house, and saw more troops hurrying toward town.

About ten o'clock many pieces of artillery and large ammunition trains came up, filling the open space to the east of us. Regiment after regiment continued to press forward. I soon engaged in the occupation of the previous day; that of carrying water to the soldiers as they passed.

How often my thoughts were anxiously fixed on my dear ones at home as the troops hurried along toward town. Were they well? Were they alive? Did I still have a home? These, with many other silent inquiries, sprang to my mind without any hope of an answer. It was impossible in the present state of affairs to expect any tidings from them.

During the early part of the forenoon my attention was called to numerous rough boxes which had been placed along the road just outside the garden fence. Ominous and dismal as was the sight presented, it nevertheless did not prevent some of the soldiers from passing jocular expressions. One of the men near by, being addressed with the remark that there was no telling how soon he would be put in one of them, replied: "I will consider myself very lucky if I *get* one."

This forenoon another incident occurred which I shall ever remember. While the infantry were passing, I noticed a poor, worn-out soldier crawling along on his hands and knees. An officer yelled at him, with cursing, to get up and march. The poor fellow said he could not, whereupon the officer, raising his sword, struck him down three or four times. The officer passed on, little caring what he had done. Some of his comrades at once picked up the prostrate form and carried the unfortunate man into the house. After several hours of hard work the sufferer was brought back to consciousness. He seemed quite a young man, and was suffering from sunstroke received on the forced march.

As they were carrying him in, some of the men who had witnessed this act of brutality remarked: "We will mark that officer for this."

It is a pretty well established fact that many a brutal officer fell in battle, from being shot other than by the enemy.

Shortly after this occurrence, and while still supplying water to the passing troops, from the pump, three officers on horseback came riding up to the gate. The centre one kindly requested me to give him a drink. I asked him to please excuse the tin cup I then held in my hand.

He replied: "Certainly; that is all right."

After he had drunk he thanked me very pleasantly. The other two officers did not wish any.

As they were about turning away, the soldiers around gave three cheers for General Meade. The one to whom I had given the drink turned his horse about, made me a nice bow, and then saluted the soldiers. They then rode rapidly away.

I asked a soldier: "Who did you say that officer was?"

He replied: "General Meade."

Some time after this several field officers came into the house and asked permission to go on the roof in order to make observations, As I was not particularly engaged at the time, and could be most readily spared, I was told to show them the way up. They opened a trap door and looked through their field-glasses at the grand panorama spread out below.

By and by they asked me if I would like to look. Having expressed my desire to do so they gave me the glasses. The sight then beheld was wonderful and sublime.

The country for miles around seemed to be filled with troops; artillery moving here and there as fast as they could go; long lines of infantry forming into position; officers on horseback galloping hither and thither! It was a grand and awful spectacle, and impressed me as being some great review.

During the whole of this afternoon Mrs. Weikert and her daughters were busy baking bread for the soldiers. As soon as one ovenful was baked it was replenished with new, and the freshly baked loaves at once cut up and distributed. How eagerly and gratefully the tired-out men received this food! They stated that they had not tasted such sweet bread for a long time. Perhaps it was because they were eating it once more on loyal soil.

It was shortly before noon that I observed soldiers lying on the ground just back of the house, dead. They had fallen just where they had been standing when shot. I was told that they had been picked off by Rebel sharpshooters who were up in Big Round Top.

Toward the middle of the afternoon heavy cannonading began on the two Round Tops just back of the house. This was so terrible and severe that it was with great difficulty we could hear ourselves speak. It began very unexpectedly; so much so, that we were all terror-stricken, and hardly knew what to do.

Some of the soldiers suggested that we had better go to a farm house about one-half a mile across the fields to the east; and acting on their advice we ran thither as fast as we could.

On our way over, my attention was suddenly attracted, in the direction of the town, to what seemed a sheet of lightning. This bright light remained in the sky quite awhile. The first thought that flashed upon my mind was, perhaps it is Gettysburg burning; and so expressed my fear to some of the soldiers we were then passing.

One of the men more bent on mischief than on sympathy, said: "Yes, that is Gettysburg and all the people in it."

This made me cry, for I thought at once of the dear ones at home.

When we reached the farm-house some of the soldiers who were about the place, seeing me in tears, were touched with compassion, and asked the cause. I told him what had been said to me, and that my parents and sister were in the town. They assured me that in war the rule was, always to allow helpless and innocent citizens to get out of a place, and never to destroy them. I then felt comforted, and they further told me that the light I saw was some signal.

Here we were permitted to remain but a few minutes, for hardly had we arrived at our supposed place of refuge, when we were told to hurry back to where we came from; that we were in a great deal more danger, from the fact that the shells would fall just about this place, whereas at the house near Round Top the shells would pass over us. So there was no alternative but to retrace our steps about as fast as we came.

During our flight over to the farm-house, and when about half way, Mrs. Weikert happened to think of some highly prized article of dress, that in our sudden flight she had never thought of. Nothing would do but that her husband would have to go back to the house and get it. Thus in the midst of the confusion of battle, Mr. Weikert started back. Just as we were reaching our starting point, we met him coming out with the treasure; a brand-new quilted petticoat; and we all went panting into the house.

During the whole of this wild goose chase, the cannonading had become terrible! Occasionally a shell would come flying over Round Top and explode high in the air over head. Just before leaving so hurriedly, a baking had been put in the old-fashioned oven; when we came back we expected to find it all burned, but fortunately the soldiers had taken it out in good time. They doubtless had their eye on it as well as on the enemy.

The cannonading, which all the time appeared to be getting more and more severe, lasted until the close of day.

It seemed as though the heavens were sending forth peal upon peal of terrible thunder, directly over our heads; while at the same time, the very earth beneath our feet trembled. The cannonading at Gettysburg has already gone down into history as terrible.

Those who are familiar with this battle now know what havoc and destruction were accomplished on this afternoon, on the west side of the Round Tops, at Devil's Den, Sherby's Peach Orchard and the Wheatfield.

During the heavy firing of which I have just spoken, and while Mr. Weikert was in the house searching for the treasure heretofore mentioned, he heard something heavy fall inside the enclosed stairway. Suddenly the door was burst open, when out rolled the poor soldier who had been wrapped in cotton. He had become terrified at the heavy peals of artillery, and springing from his bed in his blindness, groped around, trying to find the stairs. He was again carried up and after that someone remained with him. This occurrence delayed Mr. Weikert in returning to us across the fields, and hence it was that we met him just leaving the house on our return.

Between four and five o'clock in the afternoon, I heard some of the soldiers about the house saying: "The Rebels are on this side of Round Top, coming across the fields toward the house, and there will be danger if they get on the Taneytown road."

Just then some one said that the Pennsylvania Reserves were on the way, and having a brother in the First Regiment of the Reserves I was anxious to see whether he would be along.

As I went out to the south side of the house I looked in the direction of Round Top, and there saw the Rebels moving rapidly in our direction.

Suddenly I heard the sound of fife and drum coming from the other side of the barn.

Then some of our soldiers shouted!: "There come the Pennsylvania Reserves!" And sure enough there they were, coming on a double-quick between the barn and Round Top, firing as they ran.

CHARGE OF THE PENNSYLVANIA RESERVES

On this evening the number of wounded brought to the place was indeed appalling. They were laid in different parts of the house. The orchard and space around the buildings were covered with the shattered and dying, and the barn became more and more crowded. The scene had become terrible beyond description.

That night, in the house, I made myself useful in doing whatever I could to assist the surgeons and nurses. Cooking and making beef tea seemed to be going on all the time. It was an animated and busy scene. Some were cutting bread and spreading it, while I was kept busy carrying the pieces to the soldiers.

One soldier, sitting near the doorway that led into a little room in the southeast corner of the basement, beckoned me to him. He was holding a lighted candle in his hand, and was watching over a wounded soldier who was lying upon the floor. He asked me if I would get him a piece of bread, saying he was very hungry. I said certainly, ran away and soon returned. I gave him the bread and he seemed very thankful. He then asked me if I would hold the light and stay with the wounded man until he came back. I said I would gladly do so, and that I wanted to do something for the poor soldiers if I only knew what. I then took the candle and sat down beside the wounded man. I talked to him and asked if he was injured badly.

He answered: "Yes, pretty badly."

I then asked him if he suffered much, to which he replied: "Yes, I do now, but I hope in the morning I will be better."

I told him if there was anything I could do for him I would be so glad to do it, if he would only tell me what. The poor man looked so earnestly into my face, saying: "Will you promise me to come back in the morning to see me."

I replied: "Yes, indeed." And he seemed so satisfied, and faintly smiled.

The man who had been watching him now returned, and thanked me for my kindness. I gave him the light and arose to leave.

The poor wounded soldier's eyes followed me, and the last words he said to me were: "Now don't forget your promise."

I replied: "No indeed," and expressing the hope that he would be better in the morning, bade him good night.

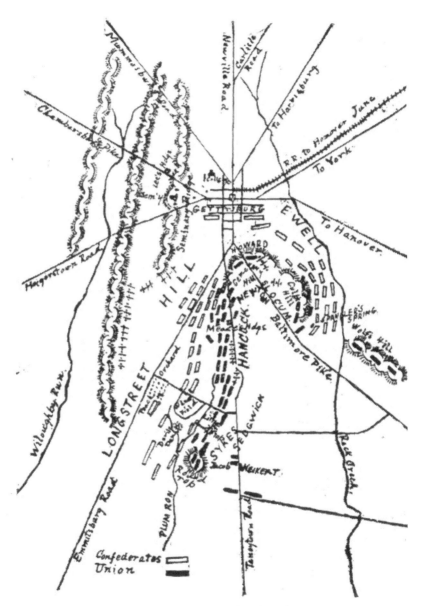

MAP OF THE THIRD DAY'S BATTLE.

CHAPTER V

DURING THE THIRD DAY OF THE BATTLE

The sun was high in the heavens when I awoke the next day. The first thought that came into my mind, was my promise of the night before.

I hastened down to the little basement room, and as I entered, the soldier lay there – dead. His faithful attendant was still at his side.

I had kept my promise, but he was not there to greet me. I hope he greeted nearer and dearer faces than that of the unknown little girl on the battle-field of Gettysburg.

As I stood there gazing in sadness at the prostrate form, the attendant looked up to me and asked: "Do you know who this is?"

I replied: "No sir."

He said: "This is the body of General Weed; a New York man."

As concerning many other incidents of the late war, so with the death of this brave general, I find an erroneous judgment has been formed; some claiming that he was instantly killed on Little Round Top, during the fight of the second day.

That General Weed was mortally wounded on Little Round Top while assisting at Hazlett's battery on account of the scarcity of gunners, is well established. That Lieutenant Hazlett was instantly killed, while bending over the prostrate form of his commander to catch his dying message, is also undisputed; but that General Weed *died* on Little Round Top is a mistake.

What is more likely than, that after being severely wounded, he should be taken down the eastern slope of the hill, away from the conflict, reaching the Taneytown road at its base? What more probable than, on reaching that road that they should carry his body away from the field by going toward the south? Why would they *not* carry him into Mr. Weikert's house when that was the first place they reached, that was used as a battle hospital?

Doubtless General Weed was carried from the field as dead, but the place and circumstances of his death, are given in the preceding lines.

I could never forget that name, and always remembered it by reason of the similarity of sound with that of General Meade, whom I had also seen that same day, when I handed him a drink.

But to return to the passing events.

Tired-out with the strain and exciting scenes of the previous day, I was still sound asleep when the family had finished breakfast; so that when I got down stairs all traces of the morning meal had been cleared away.

While in conversation with the soldier beside the body of General Weed, as above related, I was told by some one, that the carriages were in waiting out at the barn, to take us off to a place of safety.

Already there was occasional musketry and cannonading in the direction of Gettysburg, and we expected greater danger than at any time before.

Some of the soldiers told us that they had planted cannon on two sides of the house, and that if the Rebels attempted to reach the Taneytown road, as they had the day before, there would likely be hard fighting right around the house; and that if we remained, we would be in the midst of flying bullets and shell. Under these circumstances we made all possible haste to depart.

When we reached the carriages, and were about to get in, a shell came screaming through the air directly overhead. I was so frightened that I gave a shriek and sprang into the barn. Even with their suffering, the poor fellows could not help laughing at my terror and sudden appearance. One of them near me said: "My child, if that had hit you, you would not have had time to jump." Pretty sound logic. Just after I jumped into the barn, I noticed that the shell had struck in the adjoining field, without exploding.

We then got into the carriages as quickly as possible, and started for a place of safety.

A short distance below the barn we came to quite a number of troops, who were drawn up in line as if held in reserve. Upon inquiry, we were informed that they belonged to the Sixth Corps.

After proceeding a mile or so down the Taneytown road, we turned to the left and crossed over to the Baltimore Pike, near the Two Taverns.

Between the Taneytown road and the Baltimore pike, we passed through a strip of woods, where, some of the soldiers told us, there had been a cavalry fight just an hour previous. Here I first saw Rebel prisoners; there was a whole field filled with them. Their appearance was very rough, and they seemed completely tired out.

While we were talking with our soldiers, I noticed one eating a "hard tack". I, having had nothing to eat as yet that day, and being quite hungry, must have looked very wistfully at him, for he reached into his haversack and presented me with one of those army delicacies. I accepted it with thanks, and nothing that I can recall was ever more relished, or tasted sweeter, than that Union soldier's biscuit eaten on July 3, 1863.

We finally arrived at a farm house beyond the pike, and found the place full of people who had also fled from their homes, to get beyond the dangers of the battle.

Toward the close of the afternoon it was noticed that the roar of the battle was subsiding, and after all had become quiet we started back for Mr. Weikert's home. As we drove along in the cool of the evening, we noticed that everywhere confusion prevailed. Fences were thrown down near and far; knapsacks, blankets and many other articles, lay scattered here and there. The whole country seemed filled with desolation.

Upon reaching the place I fairly shrank back aghast at the awful sight presented. The approaches were crowded with wounded, dying and dead. The air was filled with moanings, and groanings. As we passed on toward the house, we were compelled to pick our steps in order that we might not tread on the prostrate bodies.

When we entered the house we found it also completely filled with the wounded. We hardly knew what to do or where to go. They, however, removed most of the wounded, and thus after a while made room for the family.

As soon as possible, we endeavored to make ourselves useful by rendering assistance in this heartrending state of affairs. I remember that Mrs. Weikert went through the house, and after searching awhile, brought all the muslin and linen she could spare. This we tore into bandages and gave them to the surgeons, to bind up the poor soldier's wounds.

By this time, amputating benches had been placed about the house. I must have become inured to seeing the terrors of battle, else I could hardly have gazed upon the scenes now presented. I was looking out one of the windows facing the front yard. Near the basement door, and directly underneath the window I was at, stood one of these benches. I saw them lifting the poor men upon it, then the surgeons sawing and cutting off arms and legs, then again probing and picking bullets from the flesh.

Some of the soldiers fairly begged to be taken next, so great was their suffering, and so anxious were they to obtain relief.

I saw the surgeons hastily put a cattle horn over the mouths of the wounded ones, after they were placed upon the bench. At first I did not understand the meaning of this but upon inquiry, soon learned that that was their mode of administering chloroform, in order to produce unconsciousness. But the effect in some instances was not produced; for I saw the wounded throwing themselves wildly about, and shrieking with pain while the operation was going on.

To the south of the house, and just outside of the yard, I noticed a pile of limbs higher than the fence. It was a ghastly sight! Gazing upon these, too often the trophies of the amputating bench, I could have no other feeling, than that the whole scene was one of cruel butchery.

But I do not desire to dwell upon such pictures any longer, for they are the most horrible that the battle presented to my mind.

Twilight had now fallen; another day had closed; with the soldiers saying, that they believed this day the Rebels were whipped, but at an awful sacrifice.

CHAPTER VI

AFTER THE BATTLE

It was the Fourth of July, and never has the cheering on that anniversary been more hearty and welcome than it was in 1863.

On the summits, in the valleys, everywhere we heard the soldiers hurrahing for the victory that had been won. The troops on our right, at Culp's Hill, caught up the joyous sound as it came rolling on from the Round Tops on our left, and soon the whole line of blue, rejoiced in the results achieved. Many a dying hero's last breath, carried a thanksgiving and praise to Him, who had watched over, and directed the thoughts and movements of the last three days. Most befitting was it, that on the fourth of July, an overruling and allwise Providence should again declare this people, free and independent of the tyranny upheld by an enemy. Again had our natal day been recognized and honored by vouchsafing a new and purified existence to our nation, whose very life had been trembling on the brink of destruction, during this terrible ordeal.

We were all glad that the storm had passed, and that victory was perched upon our banners.

But oh! the horror and desolation that remained. The general destruction, the suffering, the dead, the homes that nevermore would be cheered, the heart-broken widows, the innocent and helpless orphans! Only those who have seen these things, can ever realize what they mean.

May the heart of this fair land be forever inclined unto wisdom, so that we may never fall into the folly of another war, and be compelled to pay the fearful penalty that is sure to follow.

For a number of days after the battle, amputating, nursing and cooking continued on the premises, after which the wounded were removed to the different corps' hospitals. During this time many a brave and noble spirit went from its tenement, and passed to the great beyond. This is what it meant, when they silently carried out a closed rough box, placed it upon a wagon and drove away.

A day or so after the battle, a soldier approached me and spoke as though he were acquainted. His face seemed familiar, yet I could not just then remember of ever having met him; whereupon he asked me if I did not recollect the soldier who got me on the wagon during the first day's fight. I then recognized him, and was very glad to greet him once again, and to express my thanks for his kindness. Before leaving, he presented me with a relic, it being a button which he cut from a Confederate's coat, to which was attached a piece of the gray cloth. I have it yet, and is one of my most highly prized relics of those thrilling days.

During the battle I met a captain of artillery, who occasionally came to Mr. Weikert's house. He was a kind, pleasant and intelligent man whose very countenance told me that he possessed a soul of honor and sympathy, and which at once inspired a confidence. As soon as he learned that my residence was in Gettysburg, and knew how concerned I was about my home folks, he kindly told me that he would do his very best to visit them, and acquaint them of my safety. I then told him how he could find the place, by noticing a row of Linden trees standing in front of a double brick house and by other indications.

He came to the place every day, saying he had been to see my mother, thus trying to cheer me. I always detected that he had not been there, for when I asked him to tell me the number of trees standing in front of the house, or give me some other assurance, he invariably failed. Then he would encourage me by saying he would go there just as soon as he could get into the town.

On the evening of the 4th, this captain came into the basement kitchen, where, in company with a number of surgeons and nurses, I was sitting at a table, eating supper. He hurried to me and said: "Now *this* time I was at your mother's."

I again began my usual inquiries, how many trees in front of the house, etc., to which he replied: "I don't care how many trees there are, but to convince you, your mother told me all about your horse being stolen, and that Jennie Wade had been killed while baking bread for her sick sister."

"I soon learned from the conversation, that he had been to my home, and had seen and conversed with my parents and sister. I felt very grateful to him for his kindness, as it was a great comfort to know that no harm had befallen them, and that he had conveyed to them the happy intelligence of my safety.

Should any of those who sat around the table that evening be still living, they will doubtless recall the conversation between that little girl and the artillery captain. I can still see how they laughed at and twitted the captain on account of the searching questions I put to him.

I saw this friend a few times afterwards, then he was gone, I hope he passed safely through the war, is still living, and will remember the incident I have just narrated.

On the following day, July 5th, I accompanied Beckie Weikert and her friend, Lieutenant George Kitzmiller of the First Pennsylvania Reserves, and whom she afterwards married, on a trip to Little Round Top.

As the Lieutenant's company was raised from our town, and as one of my brothers was a member of the company, I eagerly inquired whether he also had been in this battle. He informed me that my brother had been taken very sick on the Peninsula, and was still in the hospital at Washington. It was a great satisfaction to know he was still living, though I was very sorry to hear of his sickness.

While we were climbing up Little Round Top we met one of the Pennsylvania "Buck Tails", who walked with us and pointed out the different places where the bodies lay among the rocks.

By this time the Union dead had been principally carried off the field, and those that remained were Confederates.

As we stood upon those mighty bowlders, and looked down into the chasms between, we beheld the dead lying there just as they had fallen during the struggle. From the summit of Little Round Top, surrounded by the wrecks of battle, we gazed upon the valley of death beneath. The view there spread out before us was terrible to contemplate! It was an awful spectacle! Dead soldiers, bloated horses, shattered cannon and caissons, thousands of small arms. In fact everything belonging to army equipments, was there in one confused and indescribable mass.

Here again, I had the advantage of a field glass, for there were also some officers present who kindly gave me an opportunity of thus viewing the field.

Little Round Top overlooking the scene of Pickett's Charge (LC)

On account of the confusion everywhere abounding, and the impassable condition of the roads, it was thought best for me to remain at Mr. Weikert's for several days after the battle, and especially since my folks knew I was safe.

Sometime during the forenoon of Tuesday, the 7th, in company with Mrs. Schriver and her two children, I started off on foot to reach my home. As it was impossible to travel the roads, on account of the mud, we took to the fields. While passing along, the stench arising from the fields of carnage was most sickening. Dead horses, swollen to almost twice their natural size, lay in all directions, stains of blood frequently met our gaze, and all kinds of army accoutrements covered the ground. Fences had disappeared, some buildings were gone, others ruined. The whole landscape had been changed, and I felt as though we were in a strange and blighted land. Our killed and wounded had by this time been nearly all carried from the field. With such surroundings I made my journey homeward, after the battle.

We finally reached and passed through the Evergreen Cemetery, and beheld the broken monuments and confusion that reigned throughout that heretofore peaceful and silent city of the dead. We passed out through the now shattered archway of the lodge, stood awhile to look at the barricade and battery on the Baltimore pike, and the wrecks and confusion extending over to Culp's Hill. After a few minutes more walk we reached our homes.

I hastened into the house. Everything seemed to be in confusion, and my home did not look exactly as it did when I left. Large bundles had been prepared, and were lying around in different parts of the room I had entered. They had expected to be compelled to leave the town suddenly. I soon found my mother and the rest. At first glance even my mother did not recognize me, so dilapidated was my general appearance. The only clothes I had along had by this time become covered with mud, the greater part of which was gathered the day on which we left home.

They had not been thinking just then of my return. My sudden appearance, and the sad plight I was in, were the cause of their not recognizing me at once. There was no girl at Mr. Weikert's of my size, hence it was impossible to furnish me with other clothes, even had they had the time to think of such a thing.

As soon as I spoke my mother ran to me, and clasping me in her arms, said: "Why, my dear child, is that you? How glad I am to have you home again without any harm having befallen you!"

I was soon told that my clothes were still down in the cellar on the wood pile, just where I had put them, and that I should go at once and make myself presentable.

For many days, I related to the ones at home, and to others who had heard of my adventures, the scenes and trials through which I had passed during my absence. Those at home, also, had many interesting and thrilling experiences to narrate, to the recital of which the next chapter will be principally devoted.

CHAPTER VII

HOME

Sometime after the battle had commenced, my father went down street, he having heard that the wounded were being brought to the warehouses located in the Northern part of the town.

Desiring to assist all he could, he remained there, working for the poor sufferers until pretty late in the afternoon.

Some of the wounded had been piteously calling and begging for liquor in order to deaden the pain which racked their bodies. Father, knowing that the dealers had removed that article out of town, said he would go to some private parties, and try to obtain it. His search however was fruitless, as no one seemed to have any.

It was while thus moving around on this errand, that he noticed our men were fast retreating through the streets, and hurrying in the direction of the Cemetery.

Knowing that his family were alone, he concluded it was best to hasten to them.

On his way home, he stopped for a few minutes at a place just a square west of our house, on some business he wished to attend to. When he came out, there was no sign of Union soldiers.

As he was approaching his home, he noticed a Rebel crossing the street, a short distance beyond. He looked at my Father who was entirely alone, stopped, and halloed: "What are you doing with that gun in your hand?" Father, who was in his shirt sleeves, threw up his arms and said: "I have no gun!" Whereupon the Confederate deliberately took aim and fired.

As soon as Father saw him taking aim, he threw himself down, and had no sooner done so, when he heard the "zip" of the bullet. In the parlance of to-day, that would be styled "a close call."

The murderous Rebel passed on; no doubt concluding that he made one Yankee the less.

As soon as he had passed down Baltimore Street, Father got up, and had almost reached the house, when he was spied and overtaken by a squad of five Confederates coming down an alley, and who greeted him by saying: "Old man, why ain't you in your house?"

He replied that he was getting there just as fast as he could. They however commanded: "Fall in!"

He certainly did so, and accompanied them until he reached the front porch, when he stepped up and said: "Now boys, I am home, and I am going to stay here."

They did not insist on taking him along, but demanded to search the house for Union soldiers; to which Father replied: "Boys you may take my word for it; there are no Union soldiers in the house." They believed him and passed on.

While he was sitting on the porch, several other squads of Rebels passed. These also wanted to search the house; some even threatening to break the door open. They were however persuaded to desist, on being told by Father, that it was against the rules of war to break into private houses; that he knew the family were very much frightened: and that he would give his word for it, that there were no Union soldiers in the house.

One of the Confederates then exclaimed: "Boys, I take that gentleman's word."

"By the way, what are your proclivities?" asked one of the men. Father replied: "I am an unconditional Union man; and to back it up, I am a whole-souled one."

One of the group then replied: "Well, we like you all the better for that; for we hate the milk and water Unionists."

Before leaving, they told Father, that he had better get into the house, that *they* would not shoot him, but that he was in danger of being shot by his own men, since the Union sharp-shooters out by the Cemetery, were already sending their bullets pretty fast in that direction.

Finding the front, as well as all the other doors securely locked, he was obliged to enter the house by the back cellar door.

After he got in, imagine his surprise and consternation, after what he had just been telling, to find no less than five Union soldiers in the house. They were all sick and disabled; two of them were captains, and were very badly wounded.

Mother nursed them and dressed their wounds during all the time of the battle. Often would they express their gratitude for her kindness and attention.

As a rule the folks stayed in the cellar during the day, as that was considered the safest place, and it was only at night after the firing had ceased, that they ventured up into the house. Very little undisturbed sleep did they enjoy during those nights.

We never heard from the five wounded men who had been nursed in the house, except that after a period of twenty-five years, one of them returned and made himself known.

It was on the first of July, 1888, exactly twenty-five years from the time he retreated into our house, that the same soldier, with his little son, stopped at the front door, and asked if the family was still living there that had been during the battle. He was informed that the only one left of those who nursed him was my father, now in his eighty third year. We told him that the kind mother who dressed his wounds and waited on him was no more on earth, and that my sister, who also assisted, had preceded her some years.

He felt quite disappointed at not meeting his kind benefactresses, but was still glad to meet and talk with my father, of the thrilling times they had spent together in different parts of the house.

He related to us his experiences, among which he told, how, during one night the Rebels came up into the house from the cellar. Hearing them come, he crawled under a settee that was standing in the hall. This settee had curtains around the lower part of it, which thus concealed him from sight. He said the Rebels passed right by him, and he heard them wondering if there were any Yankees in the house. They did not go any further than the hall and soon returned to the cellar. He assured us that he took a good, long sigh of relief after they had gone down and out, the way they came in.

This soldier was Corporal Michael O'Brien, of Co. A., 143rd Pennsylvania Volunteers, 1st Corps. He enlisted at Wilkes-Barre, Pa., and at the time of the visit referred to above, was a resident of Waverly, Tioga County, N.Y. He said he had been wounded during the first day's engagement, by a ball striking him in the back, and then passing to his right arm, shattering it at the elbow. We all took occasion to examine his arm, and found it wasted away almost to the bone.

Another of the five wounded was a captain of the 6th Wisconsin regiment, but his name I do not know.

This is all the account I am able to give of the Union soldiers concealed, nursed and protected in our house during the battle.

Mother always called them her boys, and often wondered what had become of them. It may be that Corporal O'Brien was the only one of them who survived the war.

Through the night of the first day of the fight, my father was frequently up in the garret; and from the window looking out toward the Cemetery Hill, could distinctly hear our troops chopping, picking and shoveling, during the silent hours. Our men were busy forming their line of breastworks, preparatory to meeting the enemy on the morrow.

At different times while the battle was going on, my father, accompanied by some of the soldiers in the house, went to the garret in order to look at the fighting out on the hill.

While thus viewing the battle, they noticed, on one occasion, in the garret of the adjoining neighbor, a number of rebel sharpshooters, busy at their work of picking off our men in the direction of Cemetery Hill.

The south wall of this house, had a number of port holes knocked into it, through which the Rebels were firing at our men. All at once one of these sharp-shooters threw up his arms, and fell back upon the garret floor. His comrades ran quickly to his assistance, and for the time being, they appeared greatly excited, and moved rapidly about. A short time afterward they carried a dead soldier out the back way, and through the garden.

On account of this position occupied by the rebel sharpshooters, a continual firing was drawn toward our house; and to this day no less than seventeen bullet holes can be seen on the upper balcony. One of the bullets cut a perfectly even hole through a pane of glass. The back porch down stairs, the fences and other places, were also riddled; showing how promptly and energetically the Union boys replied, when once they detected the whereabouts of the enemy.

The greatest wonder is, that our men did not send a shell into that house, after they detected the rebel firing.

The sharpshooters on this part of the field, had their headquarters on the north of our house; it being at the nearest corner to the line of battle, and served as quite a protection to them.

At night, when all the folks had gone up stairs, these sharpshooters would enter the cellar in search of eatables. On these occasions, as was observed from the windows above, they carried milk and cream crocks, preserves, canned fruit, etc., out into the side street; and seating themselves on the pavement, and along the gutter, no doubt had an enjoyable feast, and a hilarious time over the provisions they had captured. They did not call it stealing in war times.

One day these same men, wanted my mother to come up out of the cellar, and cook for them. She most positively declined; saying she would not dare to do it for her own family at such a time, and much less would she do it for them.

Had she complied with the request, she very likely would have lost her life; for it was just about that time, that bullets were passing through the kitchen, over and around the stove. Bullets came through the south side of the room, striking, and sometimes passing through the opposite side. Had anyone been standing in front of the stove or near it, they would have been in the line of the deadly missiles, and death would have been almost certain.

During the first day's battle, and after our men had retreated, a little girl was standing at the second story window of the house opposite ours. She had the shutters bowed, and was looking down into the street at the confusion below. Suddenly a shell struck the wall just beside the shutter, tearing out a large hole and scattering pieces of brick, mortar and plastering all around the room in which the little girl was standing. It entered and struck some place in the room, rebounded and fell out into the street.

Another ball is now placed in the wall, to mark the place where the first one struck. I am here reminded of the fact that many persons while walking or riding past this place, and having their attention called to this shell sticking in the wall, neatly encased in brick and mortar, think that it has been there just as it arrived on the first day of the battle. Shells were not quite so tidy in introducing themselves at that time.

The little girl who had the narrow escape referred to, was Laura Bergstresser, a daughter of the then Methodist minister at Gettysburg. She is now deceased.

So terrified was she at what had happened that she ran over to our house for safety. The soldiers in the house told her that it was a stray shot and might never happen again. Being assured that she was just as safe at her own home, she ran back to her parents.

When this shell struck, a brother of the little girl, lay in a room close by, very low with Typhoid fever. Through the open doors he saw it enter and go out of the building.

It was Saturday morning, after the battle, when there was a ring of the front door bell. It was the first time the bell had rung since the conflict commenced. No one ventured out on the street during those three days, fearing that they might be picked off by sharp-shooters. Hearing the ringing, mother said: "Oh! must we go and open the front door?" For she thought the battle would again be renewed. They however opened the door, and to their surprise the Methodist minister stood before them. He exclaimed: "Don't you think the rascals have gone?"

Father was so overjoyed, that not taking time to consider, ran out just as he was, intending to go to the Cemetery Hill and inform our men of the good news.

He had gone about half a square from the house, when, on looking down, saw that he was in his stocking feet. He thought to himself: "No shoes! No hat! No coat! Why, if I go out looking this way, they will certainly think that I am demented!"

He turned to go back, and while doing so saw a musket lying on the pavement. He picked it up, and just then spied a Rebel running toward the alley back of Mrs. Schriver's lot. Father ran after him as fast as he could and called: "Halt!"

The fellow then threw out his arms, and said: "I am a deserter! I am a deserter!" To which father replied: "Yes, a fine deserter you are! You have been the cause of many a poor Union soldier deserting this world; fall in here." He obeyed; and as father was marching him toward the house, he spied two more Confederates coming out of an adjoining building, and compelled them to "fall in."

These also, claimed to be deserters; but the truth is, they were left behind, when Lee's army retreated. He marched the three men out to the front street, and as there were some Union soldiers just passing, handed his prisoners over for safe keeping.

He then went into the house; put on his shoes and hat; took his gun and went up to the alley back of our lot. There he saw a Rebel with a gun in hand, also trying to escape. Father called on him to halt. The fellow faced about, put his gun on the ground, rested his arms akimbo on it, and stood looking at him. Father raised his musket, and commanded: "Come forward, or I'll fire!"

The Confederate immediately came forward and handed over his gun. On his way to the front street with this prisoner he captured two more and soon turned these over to our men.

Father then examined his gun for the first time; and behold! it was empty.

A few days after the battle, several soldiers came to our house and asked mother if she would allow them to bring their wounded Colonel to the place, provided they would send two nurses along to help wait on him, saying they would like to have him kept at a private house.

As we had a very suitable room she consented.

The wounded officer was carried to the house on a litter, and was suffering greatly. After they got him up stairs, and were about placing him on the bed, it was found to be too short, so that the foot-board had to be taken off and an extension added. The Colonel was a very tall man and of fine proportions.

He had been severely wounded in the right ankle and shoulder, the latter wound extending to his spine.

The surgeons wanted to amputate his foot, saying it was necessary in order to save his life; but the Colonel objected, and said that if his foot must go he would go too.

Mother waited on him constantly, and the nurses could not have been more devoted.

He was highly esteemed by all his men, many of whom visited him at the house, and even wept over him in his suffering and helplessness. They always spoke of him as one of the bravest men in the army.

Before long his sister came, who with tender care and cheering words no doubt hastened his recovery.

Several months elapsed before he was able to be removed; when, on a pair of crutches, he left for his home in St. Paul. As he was leaving the house he could hardly express fully, his thanks and appreciation for all our kindness; and on parting kissed us all, as though he were bidding farewell to his own kith and kin. We, on our part, felt as though one of our own family were leaving. He promised that whenever able he would come back to see us.

About three years after the battle, I was standing on the front pavement one day, when a carriage suddenly stopped at the front door. A gentleman alighted, came up to me, shook hands, and kissed me without saying a word. I knew it was the Colonel by his tall, manly form.

He ran up the front porch, rang the bell, and on meeting the rest of the family, heartily shook hands, and greeted mother and sister with a kiss.

We were all glad to meet each other again, and we earnestly desired him to stay. He however said his time was limited, and friends were waiting in the carriage to go over the battlefield. So we were forced to again say farewell.

The officer of whom I have just written, was Colonel William Colvill, of the First Minnesota Regiment. At the present writing his residence is in the city of Duluth, Michigan.

It was during the terrible struggle out by the Wheat Field, toward the close of the second day, when the confusion of the battle was confounding; when the contending columns had become mixed with each other on account of the dense smoke, when one of Wilcox' Regiments came unnoticed in contact with Humphrey's left, that General Hancock orders Colonel Colvill to "Forward" with his regiment.

The encounter is a desperate one. Many of the brave First Minnesota are slain in the hand to hand struggle; but the enemy is driven back with losses equally severe. During this engagement the Colonel received the wounds to which I have referred.

I have since learned, that out of 262 men comprising this regiment at Gettysburg, but 47 remained after this daring charge.

When Colonel Colvill and his attendants left our house, one of the men who had been nursing him, presented me with a gun and bayonet, saying: "I bought it with my own money, and I give it to you; and if any one comes after it, and wants to take it from you, just tell them that the gun was bought and paid for by the soldier who gave it to you."

One of the nurses was Milton L. Bevans, musician of Co. F, 1st Minnesota Regiment, now of Hamline, Minn.; the name of the other, and the one who gave me the gun and bayonet was Walter S. Reed, private, Co. G, also of the same regiment.

Some weeks after they had left, a Provost Marshal was sent to the town, to collect all arms and accoutrements belonging to the Government.

Some one informed him, that there was a gun at our house, for it was not long before two soldiers called. I suppose I had been bragging too much about my relic.

On going to the door, they asked me whether we had a musket about the house.

I said: "Yes sir; but it is mine."

They replied that the Provost Marshal had sent them after it, and that they would have to take it.

I told them what the soldier who gave it to me had said; whereupon they expressed their sorrow, but added, that they would have to obey.

In my indignation at this treatment I said: "If they are mean enough to take the gun they can have it; but it is *my* gun."

They seemed sorry as they rode away with my highly prized treasure, and I have no reason to doubt their sincerity.

About two hours after this, I happened to go to the front door, and on looking up the street, I saw the same two soldiers returning on horse back, one of them having a gun on his shoulder.

I ran into the house, and told my sister that I actually believed they were bringing back my gun.

Instantly the bell rang, and I told her that I was ashamed to go to the door, after talking to them the way I had.

So my sister went; but the soldiers said they wanted to see me.

I went to the door and found these same men looking quite pleased as they said to me: "The Provost Marshal heard you were such a good Union girl, he has sent back your gun, and we are very happy to return it to you."

After attempting to apologize for the way I had addressed them, they said they did not blame me in the least for they knew how I must have felt at losing a gun obtained in the way I had this one. I still have it. On its stock are cut the initials P.L.W.T., a custom quite prevalent in the army. I need hardly state how greatly I prize this relic.

I have also in my possession an officer's sword and scabbard which were presented to my sister just after the battle, by a soldier named Barney M. Kline of Company C, 55th Ohio Regiment. The scabbard must have been hit by a bullet or piece of shell, as it was almost broken off near the middle. This sword and scabbard he picked up in our orchard along the Taneytown road, which place is now embraced in the National Cemetery.

For many weeks after the battle my thoughts and attention were directed to the General Hospital, located about one mile east of the town. This was a large collection of tents, regularly laid out in Camp style.

As we passed along the Camp streets we could look into the open tents, and behold the row of cots on either side. Upon these couches lay the sufferers who, a short while before, had endured the terrors of battle, and were now hovering on the verge of Eternity.

Here also were established the Christian and Sanitary Commissions, ever exerting their moral and humane influences. In their large tents, was contained almost everything that Christian civilization could suggest to meet the necessities of those who had suffered in the conflict.

As is known to many of my readers, the province of the Sanitary Commission was to provide more especially for the bodily wants; whilst that of the Christian Commission, besides supplying necessaries for the body, took an earnest interest in the welfare of the souls of the wounded and dying. The many blessings derived from these adjuncts to our army, may not be fully known now, but they shall be revealed hereafter.

Prior to the formation of this general hospital, each corps had its own, in the locality where it had fought. This was on account of the convenience in promptly gathering and caring for its wounded. After the number of patients had become reduced, these hospitals were discontinued, and each corps was assigned to its section in the general hospital.

Many sad and touching scenes were here witnessed. Many a kind and affectionate father; many a fond and loving mother; many a devoted wife faithful unto death; many a tender and gentle sister, wiped the moisture of death from the blanched forehead of the dying hero, as they eagerly leaned forward to catch the last message of love, or to hear the announcement of a victory greater than that of death.

The friends and relatives who came to minister to the wounded were, on account of the crowded condition of the hotels, compelled to ask accommodations from private citizens. In this manner quite a number were taken into our home. Most of their time was spent at the hospital, some coming back to us in the evening, and leaving as soon as possible the next morning.

I was frequently invited to accompany these visitors, and in this way often found myself by the bedside of the wounded.

One lady who was stopping at our house, I remember in particular; a Mrs. Greenly. Her son lay suffering at the hospital, and in company we frequently visited him.

One day when he was very low it was concluded that by amputating his limb his life might be spared. After the operation had been performed her son sank rapidly. At last came the words: "*Mother – Dear Mother! – Good bye! – Good – Mother!*" – and all was over. Her darling boy lay before her in the embrace of death; but a mother's tender love had traced a peaceful smile upon his countenance. As the life went out from that racked body hope and joy forsook that fond mother's heart.

Oh! that sad face and bleeding spirit, as she bade us farewell to follow the coffined remains to her far off home.

Who will dare to say that with such sacrifices upon our country's altar our national inheritance is not sacredly precious?

I shall never forget the anxious suspense of that mother. Whilst absent from her loved one, even for a few hours, her spirit knew no rest, and as soon as possible she would hurry back.

During our visits to the hospital, we became acquainted with individual soldiers. These received our special sympathies and attentions, hence our return was always looked forward to with cheering anticipations.

Having heard what they would be allowed to have, when we again returned we brought them such delicacies as were prescribed and which they seemed most to crave. Our baskets were filled with lemons, oranges, cakes, jellies, rolls and other edibles. They always seemed glad to look upon the flowers and bouquets which we invariably brought along. Many of their tents were decorated on the outside with wreaths, festoons, corps badges wrought in evergreen, and many other beautiful designs.

Our visits cheered the poor fellows, and their eager requests to "come back again soon," made us feel that we were of some use even in our feeble way.

Many of the town ladies would spend their time in reading to the wounded. This seemed to take their thoughts from their sad condition and centre them upon objects more comforting and delightful.

Frequently we attended religious services at the hospital and gladly joined in the singing. I have no doubt the soldiers fully appreciated our presence and the part we took in the exercises; for it must have made them think of their dear ones at home, and caused them to realize that they were once more among their sympathizing sisters of the North.

CHAPTER VIII

CONCLUSION

Years have come and gone since the happening of the events narrated in the preceding chapters, but they are as indelibly stamped upon my memory as when passing before me in actual reality.

The carnage and desolation, the joys and sorrows therein depicted, have all long since passed away.

Instead of the clashing tumult of battle, the groans of the wounded and dying, the mangled corpses, the shattered cannon, the lifeless charger and the confusion of arms and accoutrements, a new era of joy and prosperity, harmony and unity prevails. Where once the bloody hand of Mars blighted and killed the choicest of Nature's offspring, there Peace, with her smiles and arts has transformed the desolation into a Paradise of beauty and bloom. Where once I saw a terrible chaos I now behold a pleasing order.

The struggle between human bondage and universal freedom, the desire to destroy this government and dishonor her flag, the cruel hatred of Americans toward each other, no more blurs our fair land.

On the very spot where in their blindness they shed the blood of fratricide, I have seen the Blue and the Gray clasp hands, and in the presence of their fellow countrymen and before High Heaven, pledge their devotion to each other, and to a renewed and purified government. On this memorable ground I have seen Gens. Longstreet, Gordon, Hooker, and Sargt. Jones (who bore the colors of the 53rd Virginia, in Pickett's charge, being thrice wounded ere he fell), with many others of the Gray, standing together with Gens. Sickles, Slocum, Beaver, Curtiss and others of the Blue; and like men and true patriots freely forgive and mourn the past.

I have heard them as representatives of different parts of our land, unitedly raise their voices in thanking God that we were once more a united people with one common cause.

To enter into detail concerning the present appearance of the battle-field is not my desire. It must be seen and studied to be appreciated. Who ever can, should not fail to visit the place.

Annually it is becoming more and more beautified. The positions of the several corps and regiments are marked by the finest sculpture of which art and science are capable. Avenues are opened so that the visitor can pass all along the line of the terrible conflict and at the same time learn from the inscriptions on the beautiful monuments, who were engaged, and at what period of the battle.

The National Cemetery, wherein repose the heroic dead, has become a marvel of loveliness. Baptized with the blood of patriots, dedicated in the immortal words of Lincoln nurtured and guarded by a grateful people, this spot for all time to come cannot be other than the nation's shrine of American virtue, valor and freedom. Here will posterity receive the same inspiration that prompted their ancestors to dare, to do and to die, for the perpetuity of the inestimable blessings that shall have come down to them.

What has been done and is still doing on the battlefield of Gettysburg, shows how devoted is the heart of the American nation to the memory of those brave men, who through their loyalty were willing to suffer and to lay down their lives in order that the precious institutions of our land might not perish.

What in my girlhood was a teeming and attractive landscape spread out by the Omnipotent Hand to teach us of His goodness, has by His own direction, become a field for profound thought, where, through coming ages, will be taught lessons of loyalty, patriotism and sacrifice.

From this combined volume of nature and art, mankind will learn that human freedom and Christian civilization have ever the smiles of a kind and allwise Providence.

Studying the annals here exhibited we cannot fail to learn that: "The God of battles" is ever present, that on those memorable days at Gettysburg *"The hand of our God was upon us, and He delivered us from the hand of the enemy."*

THE END

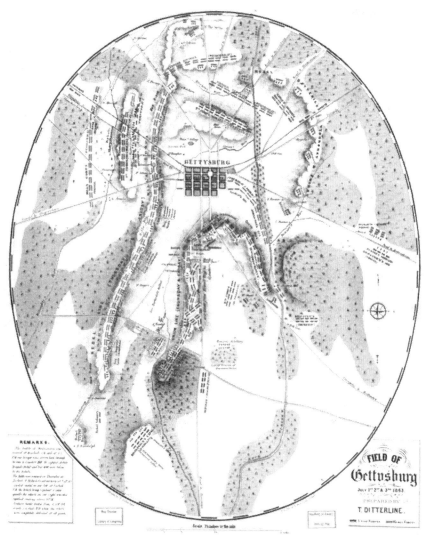

Field of Gettysburg, July 1st, 2nd, & 3rd, 1863 (LC)
Prepared by T. Ditterline

    The battle began northwest of Gettysburg on the morning of July 1st. The Union troops were driven back through town, where they rallied on the high ground. Their defensive line formed a "fish hook," allowing for a consolidated defense, better communications, and easier distribution of supplies. During "Pickett's Charge" on July 3rd, Confederates marched across the open fields southwest of town, flanked by withering fire from Union artillery on Little Round Top (the hill to the south.)

View from Cemetery Ridge (LC)

Lutheran Seminary (LC)

A Boy's Experiences During the Battles of Gettysburg

by

Daniel Skelly

With deepest affection, I dedicate
this pamphlet of reminisces
to the memory of my wife,
Lily Hill Titus Skelly,
whose devotion was
an inspiration and comfort to me
through almost a half century
of married life.

D.A.S.

Daniel Skelly, 1863

Foreword

The story of the three days which thrilled the world with the battles of the Blue and the Gray at Gettysburg placed the town necessarily in a position where the two thousand of the town played a very small alongside of the two hundred thousand of the armies. (*Editor's note: more accurately estimated numbers are Union Army 93,321 and Confederate Army 71,699.*) The history of the big army with its forced marches to get here, with its hand to hand fighting to take and to hold important positions, with the greatest cavalry fight ever waged on American soil, with its gigantic artillery duel of hours with hundreds of guns, with the magnificent charge of soldiers on foot, all the history of those days has so absorbed the attention of the world as it has been told and retold that the existence of the two thousand souls of the town seem to have been swallowed up out of sight. The writer, a boy of eighteen years, a native of the town gives in the following pages a most interesting glimpse of the life of the small town group during those three days and it is a picture well deserving preservation. He did not spend his time in the cellar where many were forced to go. He was in and through the thrilling experience of those days, hearing and seeing, and years ago he began to write the story of this time when it was all fresh in his memory and has carefully revised it from time to time. Throughout these pages there is apparent the real touch of his experiences and the life of a boy of eighteen years in Gettysburg July 1, 2, and 3, 1863, and this picture can not help but hold a wonderful fascination for every one interested in Gettysburg and everything that contributed to the story of those three great days.

Wm. Arch. McClean, Esq.

A Boy's Experiences
During the Battles of Gettysburg

The month of June 1863 was an exciting one for the people of Gettysburg and vicinity. Rumors of the invasion of Pennsylvania by the Confederate army were rife and toward the latter part of the month there was the daily sight of people from along the border of Maryland passing through the town with horses and cattle, to places of safety.

Most of the merchants of the town shipped their goods to Philadelphia for safety, as was their habit all through the war upon rumors of the Confederates crossing the Potomac. The merchandising firm in whose employ I had been for a number of years (Fahnestock Brothers) kept a car chartered and whenever these rumors reached us, day or night, we packed up the goods and sent it to Philadelphia and went out of business for the time being, until matters became settled again along the border, when the stock was brought back and we resumed our routine.

I was absent from Gettysburg in New York from the beginning of June until the latter part of the month. Leaving New York City for home on the morning of June 26, 1863, I reached Hanover, Pa., on the afternoon of that day, expecting to get a train for home from there the same evening. But about 5 o'clock the last train out of Gettysburg, until after the battle, reached Hanover filled with people getting away from the Confederates. They included revenue officers and clerks, in fact all persons who had any office under the government.

Early's Division had occupied Gettysburg that day and made demands upon the town, which were not complied with. Consequently I was obliged to remain in Hanover all night. On the morning of June 27 White's Confederate cavalry passed through Hanover and remained long enough to get some packages from the express office, one of which was for my firm and which I saw them open. It contained gloves. They appropriated them. They also captured a jeweler with his stock loaded in a wagon, who was a little late in getting started out of town, and appropriated his stock also.

On the afternoon of this day, Thaddeus Slentz, Edward Craver and myself secured a hand-car and started for Gettysburg on the Gettysburg and Hanover railroad, but when we reached New Oxford we found the bridge over the Conewago Creek had been burned by the Confederates. So we were obliged to abandon the car and walk the remaining ten miles to Gettysburg, reaching there about 5 P.M.

The 28th and 29th were exciting days in Gettysburg for we knew the Confederate army, or a part of it at least, was within a few miles of our town and at night we could see from the house-tops the campfires in the mountains eight miles west of us. We expected it to march into our town at any moment and we had no information as to the whereabouts of the Army of the Potomac. We little dreamed of the momentous events which were soon to happen right in our midst.

The town of Gettysburg in 1863 (NA)
West Middle Street runs through the center of this photograph.
The county courthouse is in the left distance on the skyline.

On June 30th two brigades of General Buford's division of cavalry reached our town, coming in from the south and I well remember how secure this made us feel. We thought surely now we were safe and the Confederate army would never reach Gettysburg.

On the afternoon of this day (the 30th) about 4 o'clock, I stood on the Cobean corner on Chambersburg Street, now occupied by Epley's Garage, while General Buford sat on his horse in the street in front of me, entirely alone, facing to the west in profound thought. I remember this incident very distinctly for it made a deep impression on me. It was the only time I ever saw the general and his calm demeanor and soldierly appearance, as well as the fact that his uniform was different from any general's I had ever seen. He wore a sort of hunting coat of blouse effect.

It is possible that from that position he was directing, through his aides, the placing of his two brigades of cavalry (Gamble's and Deven's) to the west and northwest of the town.

On the night of the 30th, the people of Gettysburg settled down in their homes with a sense of security they had not enjoyed for days and with little thought of what the morrow had in store for them.

Wednesday July 1, 1863

On the morning of July 1, about 8 o'clock, in company of my old friend Samuel W. Anderson, a resident of Kentucky, but formerly of our town (who happened to be visiting with his wife at her father's home in Gettysburg), I walked out the Mummasburg Road north of the town just a short distance beyond the college building, where lay encamped in the fields, Col. Deven's Brigade of Buford's Division of Cavalry, which with Gamble's Brigade of the same division had come into our town on the previous day. Gamble's Brigade was then encamped west of the town.

While we stood at Col. Deven's tent an order was handed him—from General Buford—directing him to move his brigade west of the town, as the Confederates were then advancing on the town by the Chambersburg Pike, west of Gettysburg.

My companion and I went directly across the fields to Seminary Ridge, then known as the Railroad Woods by reason of the "Old Tape-worm Railroad" being cut through it. Anderson went toward the Theological Seminary buildings expecting to get on the cupola of the building. I remained on Seminary Ridge just where the "Old Tape-worm Railroad" cut through it.

The ridge was full of men and boys from town, all eager to witness a brush with the Confederates and not dreaming of the terrible conflict that was to occur on that day and not having the slightest conception of the proximity of the two armies.

Seminary Ridge and the Chambersburg Road, 1863. (NA)
It was near the Lutheran Seminary building at left that Skelly
perched in a large oak tree to watch the battle west of town.

I climbed up a good-sized oak tree so as to have a good view of the ridge west and northwest of us, where the two brigades of cavalry were then being placed. We could then hear distinctly the skirmish fire in the vicinity of Marsh Creek, about three miles from our position and could tell that it was approaching nearer and nearer as our skirmishers fell back slowly toward the town contesting every inch of ground. We could see clearly on the ridge about half a mile beyond us, the formation of the line of battle of Buford's Cavalry, which had dismounted, some of the men taking charge of the horses and the others forming a line of battle, acting as infantry.

Nearer and nearer came the skirmish line as it fell back before the advancing Confederates, until at last the line on the ridge beyond became engaged. Soon the artillery opened fire and shot and shell began to fly over our heads, one of them passing dangerously near the top of the tree I was on. There was a general stampede toward town and I quickly slipped down from my perch and joined the retreat to the rear of our gallant men and boys. I started for town on the "Old Tapeworm Railroad," but crossed from it over a field to the Chambersburg Pike on the east side of Miss Carrie Shead's School and when about the middle of the field a cannon ball struck the earth about fifteen or twenty feet from me, scattering the ground somewhat about me and quickening my pace considerably.

When I reached the pike, there galloped past me a general and his staff, who upon reaching the top of the ridge, turned into the lane toward the Seminary building. This I have always believed was General Reynolds coming onto the field and going to the Seminary where he had an interview with General Buford (then on the cupola of the Seminary) before going out where the battle was in progress. The time was about 9 o'clock or near it, and our infantry had not come up yet.

I was not long in reaching town and found the streets full of men, women and children, all under great excitement. Being anxious to see more of the battle, I concluded I would go up upon the observatory on the store building of the Fahnestock Brothers, situated on the northwest corner of Baltimore and West Middle Streets, and just across the street from the court house.

Fahnestock's Store on Baltimore & West Middle Streets,
c. 1888 (Tipton Collection, NA)

The observatory was on the back of the building fronting on West Middle Street and being a three-story building had a good view of the field where the battle was then being fought. In company with Mrs. E.G. Fahnestock, wife of Col. Fahnestock, Isaac L. Johns and Augustus Bentley, I went up through the store to the observatory. There were steps from the third story floor up through the roof of the building, the exit being through a large trap door. The observatory had a railing and benches around it and was about eight feet or more square.

We had been up there quite a little time when I observed a general and his staff coming down Baltimore Street from the south of the town. Upon reaching the court house, they halted and made an attempt to get up into the belfry to make observations, but they were unable to accomplish this. I went down into the street and going over to the court house told them that if they wished they could go up on the observatory of the store building.

The general dismounted and with two of his aides went with me up onto the observatory. This was between 10 and 11 o'clock in the morning, the clock on the court house indicating the hour. Upon reaching the house-top, the general, with his field glasses, made a careful survey of the field west and northwest of the town; also of the number of roads radiating like the spokes of a wheel from the town.

In the midst of it a scout came riding up West Middle Street at a full gallop, and halting below us called up, asking if General Howard (Gen. Oliver Otis Howard, commander of the Eleventh Corps of the Army of the Potomac) were there.

General Howard answering in person, the scout called to him that General Reynolds had been killed and that he should come onto the field immediately. This scout was George Guinn, a member of Cole's Maryland Cavalry, and was from our county, a few miles below our town. I knew him well and recognized him at once.

Upon receiving this message the General, his staff officers and myself went down into the third story ware-room, when General Howard stopped and gave orders to one of his aides to ride back and meet his corps, which was then on the march from Emmitsburg, Md., ten miles from Gettysburg, and direct General (Adolph von) Steinwehr, upon reaching the field to occupy Cemetery Hill and fortify it (East Cemetery Hill). General Howard, as he came into Gettysburg, had noticed the prominence of this hill, and riding up to the cemetery was impressed with its commanding position.

To his other aide he gave some directions regarding the bringing up of his corps. One thing which he said that I remember, was that the bands should be placed at the head of the columns and play lively airs as they advanced.

General Howard was perfectly calm and self-possessed and I remember this made a lasting impression on me. And his orders became so fixed on my mind that I have never forgotten them.

Returning to Gettysburg after the war, General Howard paid a
visit to the roof of the Fahnestock Building.
The general is in the center of the group, seated on the chimney.
Daniel Skelly stands at left. (DS)

As we passed down through the house, we met Mrs.
Samuel Fahnestock, then an old lady, who was very much
agitated. The General stopped and spoke a few kindly words to
her, which relieved her anxiety considerably. He then rode out
to the front.

After General Howard left I went up on the house again,
and after some little time had elapsed we heard a commotion
down in the street (West Middle) and upon looking down saw
quite a column of Confederate prisoners, under guard of the
Boys in Blue, being conducted to the rear. It proved to be the
Confederate General Archer and several hundred of his brigade
who had been captured by the Iron Brigade.

We remained on the house-top until near noon, when it
became a little dangerous to stay longer and we went
downstairs again. But shortly after 12 o'clock another officer
came along and asked to be taken up where General Howard
had made his observations. He was a captain and belonged to
the Eleventh Corps. He only remained a short time. I learned
years after the battle that this officer's name was Frederick
Otto Baron Von Fritche, and that he had written a book
entitled "A Gallant Captain of the Civil War", in which he

made mention of my taking him up on the roof and giving him some information in regard to the field and the battle then going on.

After he had gone I walked down to our Centre Square and there met my mother carrying two buckets of water, looking for one of the improvised hospitals, to give it to the wounded. It was a striking irony of war that at that time two of my brothers, members of Company F, 87th Pennsylvania regiment, should be prisoners of war, having been captured at Winchester, Va., in an engagement while the Confederate army was on its way to Gettysburg. One of them was mortally wounded and in a southern hospital but a kind Providence withheld this from us until after the battle here.

We went down Carlisle Street to the McCurdy warehouse, just below the railroad, where the wounded were being brought in from the First Corps, then engaged west of town. No provision had yet been made for their care in the town and they were laid on the floor. We remained there quite a while giving them water and doing what we could for their relief.

The Eleventh Corps did not reach the field until after one o'clock. I stood on the Cobean corner of Chambersburg Street as Schimmelfenning's Division of the Eleventh passed through town on its way to the front. The day was hot and sultry and they were marching "quick time", all seeming eager to get to the front. All along Washington Street the people of the town were out with buckets of water and the soldiers would stop for a moment for a drink and then hurriedly catch up to their place in the line. They appeared to be straining every effort to reach the scene of conflict, and yet not an hour elapsed before the slightly wounded were limping back and those badly wounded were being brought back in ambulances to the improvised hospitals in the town. The hospitals were located in warehouses, churches, the court house and in various private homes. Many others were left dead on the field they were so heroically eager to reach such a short time before.

As the afternoon wore away the churches and warehouses on Chambersburg, Carlisle, and York Streets nearest the line of battle, were filled with wounded. Then the court house, as well as the Catholic, Presbyterian and Reformed churches and the school house in High Street received the injured soldiers, until those places had reached their capacity, when private homes were utilized, citizens volunteering to take them in and care for them.

Persons living nearest the court house, naturally gave their attention to the wounded in that building. In company with a young lady, Miss Julia Culp, a neighbor (she had a brother in the Confederate Army who was killed on Culp's Hill and a brother in the Union Army, who survived the war), I went into the court house with buckets of water and passed from one to another of the wounded relieving them as best we could under the circumstances. Some of them were so frightfully wounded that a lady could not go near them. These I gave water to, while she cared for those who were not so severely wounded. Quite a number of our townspeople were there doing everything they could in the relief work as the wounded were carried in.

When our forces were being driven back through the town in the afternoon, I went home feeling that everything was lost and throughout my life I have never felt more despondent.

One of the regiments of the Iron Brigade (I think the 19th Indiana) in falling back through town about 4 o'clock in the afternoon passed our house on West Middle street (the site of the present Kendlehart residence). As they turned into West Middle street from Washington street (at the Jacobs corner), one of the lieutenants was wounded in the foot but kept up with his regiment until he reached our house. He was unable to go any further. He came into the yard. Separating the Bowen house next door and ours, there was an areaway used by both of our families and at the Bowen house was an old-fashioned cellar door standing open. He took off his sword and pistol and sword belt.

He hobbled down with his belt and pistol and hid them in the cellar and then came up to get his sword, when the Confederates came into the yard and made him a prisoner, taking his sword away from him. My mother, standing in our kitchen doorway, seeing he was wounded, asked the Confederates to allow him to come into our house and she would care for him. They allowed him to come and then continued in pursuit of our retreating forces. My mother took him into one of the inner rooms and kept him there without the Confederates (who afterward formed a line of battle in front of four house) finding it out. After the battle he was taken to one of the hospitals. In a week or more he was convalescent and came to see is on his way to join his regiment. He sent me over to the Bowen cellar to get his accoutrements and presented them to me, saying that when he got to Washington he would get a new outfit. We never heard from him afterwards, although thousands of veterans of this engagement revisited the battlefields for years after the conflict, hunting up friends who had ministered to them when they were wounded, or looking up the locations of their regiment during the battle days. They related many interesting incidents which occurred. But our wounded visitor of the first of July, 1863, never came back.

When I went out in front of the house about 7 o'clock in the evening, the Confederate line of battle had been formed on East and West Middle streets, Rodes' Division of Ewell's Corps lying right in front of our house.

We were now in the hands of the enemy and in passing, I want to pay a tribute to these veterans of the Confederate Army. They were under perfect discipline. They were in and about our yard and used our kitchen stove by permission of my mother. They were gentlemanly and courteous to us at all times, and I never heard an instance to the contrary in Gettysburg.

We settled down quietly this night. There was no noise or confusion among the Confederate soldiers sleeping on the pavement below our windows and we all enjoyed a good night's rest after the feverish anxiety of the first day's battle.

Thursday July 2, 1863

Day dawned on the second of July bright and clear, and we did not know what to do or expect; whether to remain quietly in our homes, or go out in the town as usual and mingle with our people. But we were soon assured that if we kept within certain restrictions we could go about the town.

It was hot and sultry and the lines of battle were quiet with the exception of an occasional exchange of shots between pickets or sharpshooters. Some time during the morning in front of my home on West Middle street, not far from the court house I was in conversation with one of the Confederate soldiers, whose regiment lay along the street in line of battle, when he asked me if I had ever seen General Lee. I replied that I had not. "Well," he said, "here he comes up the street on horseback."

The general rode quietly by unattended and without any apparent recognition from the Confederate soldiers along the street. When he reached Baltimore street, about a square away at the court house, he turned into it, going up to High street. I was later informed by reliable sources that he had gone to the jail, presumably for conference, but with whom has been only surmise.

The afternoon of the second I spent in the yard back of the Fahnestock store on West Middle street. There was a high board fence the length of the lot, extending to an alley at the end. There were two large gates opening to the street along which the Confederate line ran. A Confederate major of one of the regiments was my companion. I do not remember his name or the regiment to which he belonged, but he told me he was originally from Pittsburgh, going south years before the war.

Our conversation was about the war and the causes leading up to it and the result thus far on both sides. He was a fair minded man and reasonable in his opinions, there being no rancor or bitterness evident in any of observations on the progress of the conflict. About 4 o'clock an interruption was caused in our conversation by a terrible cannonading off to the southwest of town and we separated, he joining his regiment in the street and I going to my father's house near the Fahnestock store.

Our town being in the hands of the Confederates and cut off from all communications with the outside world, we knew nothing about our army and were completely in the dark as to how it was located and how much of it had arrived on the field of battle. The Confederates maintained a clam-like silence on all matters concerning the battle, hence we did not know the significance of this tremendous cannonading until after the battle was over and the Confederates retreated. But for the present it sent everyone to the cellars as a matter of protection. (It was Longstreet's attack on Sickles' Corps and lasted until dark.)

Mr. Harvey D. Wattles lived close to my father's and under his house was a large dry cellar. During the cannonading the neighbors congregated in it as a place of safety. My mother and the rest of the family were there during the afternoon and I was there at intervals while the period of uncertainty caused by this artillery fire existed.

An incident that occurred in this house during one of these battle days will give some idea of what families were exposed to while the fighting was in progress. A neighbor had come into the house to take refuge and had brought with her a band-box containing a bonnet. When the cannonading began she went to the cellar, placing the box on the chair upon which she had been sitting. When she came from the cellar she found the box where she had left it, but a minie ball had passed through the box and the bonnet.

On the evening of the second, about dusk, Will McCreary and I were sent on some errand down on Chambersburg street and as we were crossing from Arnold's corner (now the location of the First National Bank building) to the present Eckert corner, we were halted by two Confederate soldiers who had a lady in their charge. She was on horseback and proved to be the wife of General Barlow who had come into the Confederate lines under a flag of truce looking for her husband, who had been severely wounded on July 1, and as she was informed, had been brought into the town. She informed us he was with a family "named McCreary" on Chambersburg street. We directed her to Smith McCreary's residence. (This stood on the present site of the John Spangler Property.)

She did not find the general there, however, for he had been taken from the field to the farmhouse of Josiah Benner on the Harrisburg road, just where the covered bridge crossed the creek. (It is related that the Confederate General Gordon found him on the field and had him cared for; and there is an interesting story of their meeting many after the war when General Gordon was a member of Congress and was introduced after dinner to General Barlow. Each had thought the other dead and disclosure of their identities was a great surprise to both of them.)

The night of the second I slept in a room above the Fahnestock store, with a number of other boys. This room fronted on West Middle street and had a window in it opening out to the street, with shutters which were bowed. Not making any light we would remain quietly at the window trying to catch the conversation of the Confederate soldiers who were lying on the pavement below the window. We were eager to catch something that would give us some clue to our army and how they were fairing in the battle that had been going on at intervals during the last two days, but did not learn much from them. We finally went to bed and settled down into a sound sleep as boys do who have few cares and sound health.

Friday July 3, 1863

At intervals during the night I was awakened and could hear the rattle of musketry fire off to the southeast of town, and it did not seem very far away. When we got up in the morning of the third of July this firing was a lively as during the night, with the addition of some artillery fire and continued until about 11 o'clock in the morning. About that hour I was down at my father's house and quite a number of Confederate soldiers came into the yard to the old "draw well." They were all be-grimed with powder and were "washing up." Their remarks about a hill they were butting up against were neither moral nor complimentary. Of course we were in the dark as to the cause of their discomfiture. (They were troops taken from the line of battle along the street to assist in the assault on Culp's Hill by Johnson's Division, which had gotten into our lines a short distance during the night but were repulsed and driven out about that time.)

The balance of the morning passed quietly and until about 1:30 P.M. there seemed to be a lull in the activities on the field. At least it seemed so to us, confined to the limits of the town.

About 1:30 however, pandemonium broke loose along the lines of battle and for one hour there was a din of cannonading, unprecedented on the continent. It well fitted the words of the poet:

> *Cannon to the right of us,*
> *Cannon to the left of us,*
> *Cannon in front of us,*
> *Volleyed and thundered.*

And then an ominous calm ensued. What did it mean?

We did not know. Nor could we surmise. But I ventured out cautiously from our retreat which was our place of safety during the cannonading, and walked up to the Fahnestock corner. However, I could learn nothing then about the conflict.

The alleys and street (Baltimore) leading up toward the cemetery were barricaded and the Confederate soldiers behind them in line of battle, were prepared to defend any attack from Cemetery Hill. There was a long calm, perhaps an hour, when again the artillery opened up from Cemetery Hill, all along the line of battle to the Round Tops and the rattle of musketry fire was intense then all over the line, except for intervals when great cheers went up from the mighty hosts of the Boys in Blue. But there were no rebel yells such as we had heard from time to time during the three days' battles. (This demonstration occurred, we learned later, when Pickett's charge failed.)

But we were to remain ignorant of what the great conflict of the day would bring to us, who were still in the hands of the enemy. On this night, I went to bed restless and was unable to sleep soundly. About midnight I was awakened by a commotion down in the street. Getting up I went to the window and saw Confederate officers passing through the lines of Confederate soldiers bivouacked on the pavement below, telling them to get up quietly and fall back. Very soon the whole line disappeared but we had to remain quietly in our homes for we did not know what it meant. I went back to bed but was unable to sleep.

Saturday July 4, 1863

About 4 A.M., there was another commotion in the street, this time on Baltimore, the Fahnestock building being at the corner of West Middle and Baltimore streets. It seemed to be a noisy demonstration. Going hurriedly to the window I looked out. Ye gods! What a welcome sight for the imprisoned people of Gettysburg! The Boys in Blue marching down the street, fife and drum corps playing, the glorious Stars and Stripes fluttering at the head of the lines.

They picked up the Confederate soldiers who had been left behind in the retreat and were marching them to the rear at double-quick. It was raining right briskly at this time. I got into my clothes hurriedly and went down to the front door but did not venture out. As the morning advanced, however, we went about the town mingling with our people, comparing notes and finding out how all had fared during the days we were in the hands of the enemy.

Three Confederate Prisoners (LC)

We soon learned that part of the town was still not free from "Our friends—the enemy." They had thrown up formidable breastworks extending from the Railroad Woods clear out along the ridge to Emmitsburg Road and beyond it and they were occupied by Confederate soldiers to protect the retreat of their army. As my father's house was on West Middle street, which extends in a direct line out to Haupt's Hill, which was along the embattled ridge, we were exposed during the whole day to sharpshooters' fire. (Haupt's Hill was the local name prior to the battle of that part of the ridge at the present Bream residence. It was named after Herman Haupt who conducted a ladies' school there for a number of years, long before the battle. He was a graduate of West Point and was a distinguished general during the Civil War. His wife was a daughter of the Rev. Mr. Keller, who was pastor of St. James Lutheran church here for a number of years.)

The Confederates had built little works of stone and ground, just large enough to cover their heads and protect their bodies, extending down the hill in the direction of town. And they lay behind them all day with guns loaded ready to bang away at any suspicious object in the street.

I remember that sometime during the morning several of our officers rode down the street and when about half the length of the square from Baltimore and Washington street, one of them was hit in the fleshy part of his army by a bullet, evidently causing a very painful wound, for he yelled at the top of his voice.

Sunday July 5, 1863

On this morning my friend "Gus" Bentley met me on the street and told me that down at the Hollinger warehouse (now Wolf's) where he was employed they had a lot of tobacco. "We hid it away before the Rebs came into town," he continued, "and they did not find it. We can buy it and take it out and sell it to the soldiers." (They were still in their lines of battle.)

Like all boys of those days we had little spending money but we concluded we would try and raise the cash in some way. I went to my mother and consulted her about it and she loaned me ten dollars. Gus also got ten, all of which we invested in the tobacco. It was in large plugs—Congress tobacco, a well known brand at that time. With an old-fashioned tobacco cutter we cut it up into ten cent pieces and each of us took a basket full and started out Baltimore street to the cemetery, the nearest line of battle. Reaching the Citizens Cemetery we found a battery of artillery posted there (brass guns), two of the guns across the road, one on the pavement, and the other in the middle of Baltimore pike. The soldiers stopped us and would not let us pass, their orders being not to let anyone out of the town.

We went back into the town as far as the Presbyterian church and went up High street to the jail, where we turned into a path leading down to the old Rock Creek "swimmin' hole." On the first ridge we saw the first dead Confederate soldiers lying right on the path (two of them side by side) and they were buried there afterward until the Confederate bodies were taken up years later and shipped to Richmond for burial.

We kept to the path down to the spring (now East Confederate avenue) then turned over towards Culp's Hill, ascending it at one of its steepest points. There were all kinds of debris of the battle scattered over the hill, but no dead or wounded soldiers, they having already been removed.

The breastworks were formidable looking, about three feet or more high, built of trees that had been cut down by the soldiers for the purpose of throwing up these fortifications. A shallow trench was dug in front of the works and the ground thrown up on it. The soldiers helped us over the breastworks with our baskets and in a short time they were empty and our pockets filled with ten cent pieces. The soldiers told us to go home and get some more tobacco, that they would buy all we could bring out. We made a number of trips, selling out each time, and after disposing of all our supply, and paying back our borrowed capital, we each had more money than we ever had before in our lives.

General Meade's Headquarters, soon after the battle (NA)

Monday July 6, 1863

On Monday, July 6, I made my first trip over our line of battle out to the Round Tops. Fences were all destroyed and the country all open so that we could drive or walk across country instead of having to take the Emmitsburg or Taneytown Roads. The whole countryside was covered with ruins of the battle. Shot and shell, guns, pieces of shells and bullets were strewn about the fields in every direction and everything that the carnage of battle could produce was evident.

Ziegler's Grove showed the effects of the Confederate artillery fire. Good-sized trees were knocked off and splintered in every imaginable way. The bodies of horses that had been killed were lying about.

Dead horses on the Trostle farm (LC)

The sight around Meade's headquarters along the Taneytown Road was terrible, indicating the exposed position it occupied, subject to every shot and shell that came over the ridge above it. Around the house and yard and below it lay at least 12 or 15 dead horses, shot down no doubt while aides and orderlies were delivering orders and messages to headquarters.

A short distance below the house there was a stone fence dividing a field. Across this was hanging a horse which had been killed evidently just as he was jumping the fence, for its front legs were on one side and the hind legs on the other. In the road a short distance away was another horse which had been shot down while drawing an ambulance.

In the front room of the house was a bed, the covers of it thrown back; and its condition indicated that a wounded soldier had occupied it. I was told that General Butterfield, Meade's chief of staff, who had been wounded, had been placed upon it before being taken to a hospital.

The Peter Trostle House, July 5-6, 1863 (NA)

The Trostle house was entirely deserted. In their kitchen the dinner table was still set with all the dishes from the meal, and fragments of food remained, indicating that the family had gotten up from their meal and made a hurried getaway.

On the Codori farm there were still some dead Confederates who had not been buried. They were lying on their backs, their faces toward the heavens, and burned as black as coal from exposure to the hot sun.

Confederate Dead (LC)

Confederate Graves (LC)

One of the saddest sights of the day's visit on the field I witnessed near the Devil's Den, on the low ground in that vicinity. There were twenty-six Confederate officers, ranking from a colonel to lieutenants, laid side by side in a row for burial. At the head of each was a board giving their names, ranks and commands to which they belonged. A short distance away was another group of thirteen arranged in the same way.

They had evidently been prepared for burial by their Confederate companions before they had fallen back, so that their identity would be preserved, and they would receive a respectable burial. Among the hundreds of graves on the battlefield there was but one whose headboard had the Masonic emblems on it. I saw it for the first time this day and often stopped to look at it afterward.

It was close to the southern end of the Codori barn along the Emmitsburg Road. It was the grave of a Confederate colonel. I did not know the significance of those Masonic emblems at the time, but many years afterward it was brought back to me forcibly. When the state made their appropriations for the erection of monuments to their regiments engaged in the battle, General Horatio G. Rogers, a distinguished soldier and historian, who commanded the Second Rhode Island Regiment in the battle, called upon me. (I was then secretary of the Masonic lodge here and still am.) He told me his regiment was not engaged in the battle as they were in reserve as part of the Sixth Corps, but that on the morning of July 4, they had skirmished across the Codori farm to the Emmitsburg road and that they had found the body of a Confederate colonel. Upon examination they discovered that he was a Mason and that he and all of his officers being Masons, they carried the body over to the Codori barn. There they gave it a Masonic burial as best they could, for they were virtually under a picket fire of the Confederates. I informed him that I remembered the grave well, that it had a neat paling fence around it, which was always in good condition until it was removed.

He asked me to examine our Masonic minutes to see if there was any record of the case. I did not find any reference to it. Those old Masons did not record what they were doing in such matters. But the farmer who loved there for some years after the battle told me he had put the fence around it and cared for the grave at the direction of some men in Gettysburg.

Dr. J.W.C. O'Neal had a list of all the Confederate graves on the field which were marked and the general learned from him that it was the grave of Col. Joseph Wasden, of the 22nd Georgia Regiment. Through correspondence with Georgia officials the general learned that Colonel Wasden had gone into the Confederate Army as a private and when killed was in command of the regiment. This is but one on many interesting Masonic incidents of the battle.

More than 7,800 men gave their "last full measure"
at Gettysburg (LC)

This, my first sight of a great battlefield, with all its carnage, ruin, suffering and death—and witnessed the day after the conflict—made a deep and lasting impression on my young mind, stamping war on my memory as too horrible to even think about.

As soon as the battle was over and the Confederates had retreated, our town was filled up every day by people coming from all over the country—fathers, mothers, brothers, sisters hunting their wounded or dead and the scenes on the streets near the improvised hospitals where the relatives were having their loved ones prepared for shipment by the large number of undertakers who had come into Gettysburg for the purpose, were indeed distressing.

The Christian and Sanitary Commissions came into the town with all kinds of supplies for the wounded and they did a wonderful work of relief. The Sanitary Commission took possession of the Fahnestock store, as the goods of that firm had been sent away for safety.

The room was 100 feet long and right in the center of the town. The commission filled it up with everything that could be of use to the wounded both in provisions and clothing. Consequently when my firm got their goods back the commission would not vacate at the goods remained in the car for several weeks until Col. Fahnestock, a member of the firm, came home from the army, when the commission was compelled to vacate.

During this time I roamed over the battlefield daily and the sights of havoc on the field were terrible. Wherever there was a bit of woods which had been in direct line of artillery fire of both sides, good-sized trees were knocked off, splintered and branches thrown in every direction.

Amputation being performed in a hospital tent,
Gettysburg, July 1863 (NA)

Emergency hospitals were set up on the field. Surgeons were busy at work with the restricted equipment at their command, performing the necessary amputations among the severely wounded men remaining in the hospital. The desperately wounded being cared for, many of them dying and being carried away for burial, or friends taking charge of their bodies. The gruesome scenes around these hospitals with the doctors and surgeons struggling courageously to cope with the great tasks with the limited facilities at their disposal, were terrible to contemplate.

Soon, however, the General Hospital was established in Wolf's Woods (the sight of the present dance pavilion a mile east of Gettysburg on the Lincoln Highway) and the wounded of both the Union and Confederate forces were taken there and cared for until they were able to be removed from Gettysburg, when they were sent to other hospitals. This hospital was continued until the weather commenced to get cold, when it was closed.

There was a little burial ground just on the ridge back of the woods and a number of dead on both sides were buried there side by side, until they were removed sometime later to other cemeteries.

As the wounded became convalescent, with the assistance of the nurses and others connected with the hospital, they gave occasional concerts at night, taking up small collections. They were usually well attended by persons from Gettysburg.

It has always been a wonder to me that the government, when it was acquiring the historic fields upon which the battle was fought and other sections now included in the reservation, did not buy this woods, one of the most historic and sacred spots on the field.

During the several days our town was in the hands of the enemy, our wounded who had been brought in while the first day's battle was in progress and placed in churches, schools, and in many private homes, were well cared for. The people of the town responded wonderfully in this emergency service. Mothers and daughters acted as nurses in the hospitals nearest their residences, and also provided all kinds of food and delicacies for the wounded.

In the days following the battle, the firm of Fahnestock Brothers received numerous inquires about wounded soldiers who were scattered over the field in the hospitals hastily set up at points most conveniently located to take care of the casualties. With Mrs. E.G. Fahnestock, I frequently rode back and forth among these stations, either in buggy or on horseback, looking for wounded men about whom information was sought. Sometimes it was difficult to locate them. We made other trips to the hospitals in the college and seminary buildings also. Frequently on these trips were included supplies of delicacies for the men.

So it was that the people of Gettysburg assisted in every way in solving the problems that arose incident to the great battle. The months following the conflict found many extra burdens placed on the town, but there was a willing response on the part of its citizens on all occasions and the confusion that might be expected as an aftermath of such a staggering calamity was reduced to a minimum.

November 19, 1863

As the months rolled on, the movement materialized for the establishment of a burial ground where could be assembled the bodies of those who fell here. This, in a short time, brought another memorable event in the history of the town—the dedication of the present National Cemetery and the visit of President Lincoln, during which he delivered his immortal address—November 19, 1863.

On the morning of that day I stood in our Center Square in front of the old McClellan House (now the Hotel Gettysburg) in company with my boyhood and life-long friend, the late Dr. J.C. Felty. We were awaiting the formation of the procession, which was to go to the cemetery, and Mr. Lincoln, who was being entertained by Judge Wills, whose residence was on the southeast corner of the Center Square, to take his position in the column. The Square was entirely free of any building or obstruction. The old court house which had stood in the center had been taken down in 1858, when the court house on Baltimore street was erected. A flagpole which had been erected in the center of it at the outbreak of the Civil War had been cut down when the Confederates came into Gettysburg before the battle.

Our town was filled with people who had come in during the several previous days for the dedication of the cemetery. We had but four ordinary-sized hotels of a capacity such as a town of 2,300 people would require for the entertainment of visitors during ordinary occasions. These were filled to overflowing and all private houses were also filled to capacity by friends of the families and as many other visitors as could be accommodated. I was up until after midnight on November 18th and there were many people walking the streets, unable to get any accommodations for the night.

The procession the next day was formed on the four principal streets, all centering at the Square, Chambersburg street from the west, York street from the east, Carlisle street from the north and Baltimore street from the south, which led to the cemetery. The Square was occupied by Col. Ward Lamon's bodyguard for Mr. Lincoln and was drawn up in an oblong formation—open order.

Procession south from Gettysburg (GD)

When Mr. Lincoln came over from the Wills house on horseback and took his position in the center of his bodyguard, the procession started and I was separated from my friend. I followed the column on the west side of Baltimore street, remaining on the outside of the curb as the pavement was crowded with people.

When I reached the top of Baltimore Hill I caught up with Mr. Lincoln's position and kept along side of him up what is now called Steinwehr avenue, to the junction of the Emmitsburg and Taneytown roads, going almost to the rear entrance of the National Cemetery, at which point the procession turned directly to the east, where I lost my place at the President's side, but managed to get through the crowd and reach the platform which the exercises were to be held.

It was erected at or near the position now occupied by the United States monument, facing a little to the north of west. I succeeded in getting up close to the north side of it and held my position until the preliminary exercises were over and the Hon. Edward Everett had commenced his oration, when I climbed up on the side of the platform, with my feet on the floor of it, and left arm over the railing, I kept that place all through the exercises.

Frank Leslie's Illustrated Newspaper, Dec. 5, 1863 (SI)

Mr. Everett's oration was quite long, lasting perhaps and hour and a half or longer, but I listened to it attentively, for it was interesting, historical and classical, with a resume of the battle which no doubt was received from some of the prominent participants.

When Mr. Everett had finished his address there was some music; then Mr. Lincoln got up, took several steps forward and delivered his immortal address.

He spoke in a quiet, forcible and earnest manner with no attempt at oratory and as I remember it was received with very little if any applause. This will not seem strange if you consider the character of the audience and the occasion that brought them here.

The war had been going on for two years and quite a number of battles had been fought with terrible losses in killed and wounded, and at that time there seemed no prospect that there would be any let-up in the fighting until one side had been decisively victorious. There were present fathers and mothers who had lost sons in the war, brothers and sisters who had lost relatives, and sweethearts whose lovers had been killed or maimed since the war began. Could there be much applause from such an audience?

It was a prophecy and promise to the northland and to the southland and to the latter part of it a notice to the nations of the world—some of whom had been just waiting for a favorable opportunity to recognize the Southern Confederacy—that "this nation shall not perish from the earth." It was the earnest manner of its delivery that impressed me as a boy, and the scene with all its accompaniments marked itself so unmistakably on my mind that I have never forgotten it.

When the services were over Mr. Lincoln got up and walked over to where Mrs. E.G. Fahnestock was sitting (she and her husband, Col. Fahnestock, were both on the platform) and extending his hand said to her that he had noticed her all through the service and felt sure that he had met her before, but could not recall where it had been. She assured him, however, that it was the first time she had seen him.

I recall very vividly my impressions of Mr. Lincoln as I walked close to him out Steinwehr avenue. His face, lined and sad, bore traces of the tremendous worry the ordeal of war had brought on him. His expression was benign and kindly, and the strength of his character seemed to me to be evidenced in the pronounced features, a high forehead, a prominent nose and a decided chin jutting below firmly-set lips. His countenance seemed to reflect the tragedy of war and the significance of his visit to Gettysburg on that day.

In those early days of my life I was around horses daily and rode horseback a great deal, and to me Mr. Lincoln was the most peculiar-looking figure on horseback I had ever seen. He rode a medium-sized black horse, and was dressed in black and wore a black high silk hat. It seemed to me his feet almost touched the ground, but he was perfectly at ease, indicating he was at home on horseback.

During the days of the battles here and the period following, I made a great many friends whose memory I cherish. One of them was General Howard, whom I had directed to the housetop where he made observations of the field on the first day's battle. On his frequent trips back to the town he called to see me either at my business place or in my home, and this friendship lasted throughout the years until his death. He was an accomplished soldier, a thorough gentleman and a valued friend.

A kind Providence has prolonged my life far beyond the Psalmists' "three score years and ten," giving me health and strength and walking capacity beyond my age. For many years it has been my habit, in company with my life-long friend, Herman H. Mertz, every Sunday afternoon, summer and winter, weather permitting, to stroll over this historic field recalling incidents of the battle and studying the movements of the troops as gathered from military accounts of the conflict here. With my boyhood experiences as a background, I have always maintained an intense interest in the Battle of Gettysburg and as I have watched the town and its National Park grow in the esteem of the American people as one of its beloved historic shrines, the incidents of those days 68 years ago become more vivid than ever.

And like Thackeray's reminiscent old drummer in his "Chronicle of the Drum:"

We like to go sit in the sun here
The statues and monuments to see,
And to think of the deeds that were done here
In that glorious year, Sixty-Three.

Gettysburg, Penna., 1932.

An Appreciation

I would like to acknowledge with grateful appreciation the invaluable advice and assistance accorded to me by William Arch. McClean, Esq., and Mr. Herbert L. Grimm in the preparation of this booklet.

Daniel Alexander Skelly

The Gettysburg Address
By Abraham Lincoln

Four score and seven years ago our fathers brought forth on this continent, a new nation, conceived in Liberty, and dedicated to the proposition that all men are created equal. Now we are engaged in a great civil war, testing whether that nation, or any nation so conceived and so dedicated, can long endure.

We are met on a great battlefield of that war. We have come to dedicate a portion of that field, as a final resting place for those who here gave their lives that that nation might live. It is altogether fitting and proper that we should do this. But, in a larger sense, we cannot dedicate—we cannot consecrate—we cannot hallow—this ground. The brave men, living and dead, who struggled here, have consecrated it, far above our poor power to add or detract.

The world will little note, nor long remember what we say here, but it can never forget what they did here. It is for us the living, rather, to be dedicated here to the unfinished work which they who fought here have thus far so nobly advanced. It is rather for us to be here dedicated to the great task remaining before us—that from these honored dead we take increased devotion to that cause for which they gave the last full measure of devotion—that we here highly resolve that these dead shall not have died in vain—that this nation, under God, shall have a new birth of freedom— and that government of the people, by the people, for the people, shall not perish from the earth.

First page of an original copy of Abraham Lincoln's address
(NA)

Second page of an original copy of Abraham Lincoln's address
(NA)

National Cemetery Dedication, Lincoln's Arrival (LC)
The arrow indicates President Lincoln's head and top hat.

Close-up view of President Lincoln's top hat and head (top of the
crowd, center) as he arrives on horseback (LC)

President Lincoln delivering the Gettysburg Address (LC)
Above the arrow, left of center, no longer wearing his hat.

National Cemetery Gatehouse (LC)

The following maps are used with the kind
permission of cartographer Hal Jespersen,
www.posix.com/CW

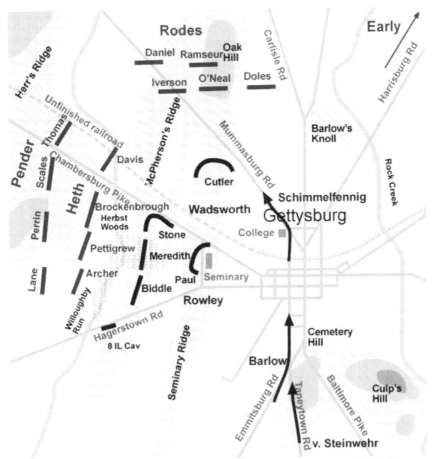

OPENING HOURS OF BATTLE OF GETTYSURG
July 1, 1863, c. 12:30 p.m.
The Confederate troops, led by Pender, Heth, and Rodes,
attacking from the north and west,
drove the Union soldiers south through the town. (HJ)

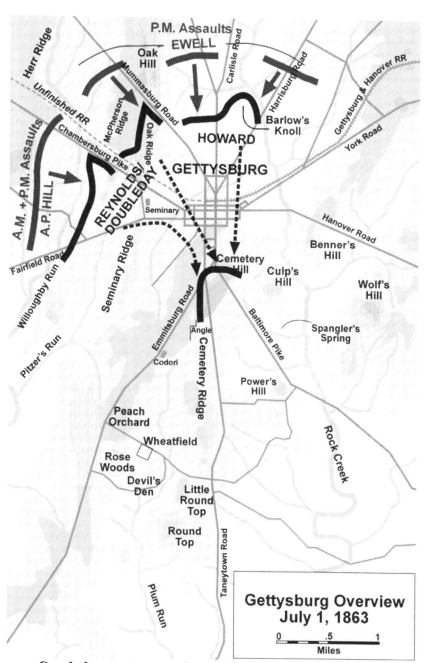

Confederate troops drove the Union Army south through town to Cemetery Ridge and Culp's Hill. (HJ)

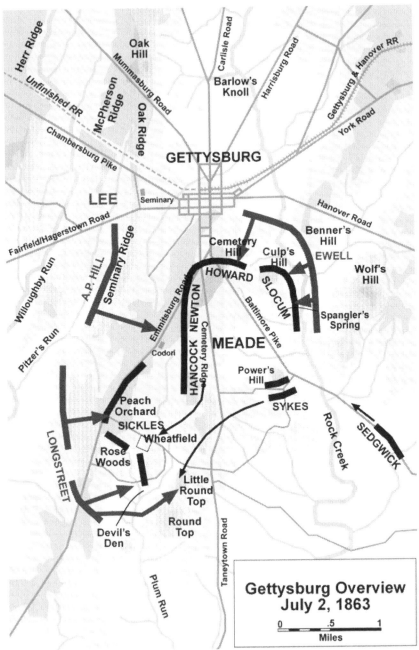

Reinforcements continued to arrive for both armies.
Union troops held a solid defensive position along
Cemetery Ridge, anchored by Little Round Top and
Culp's Hill. (HJ)

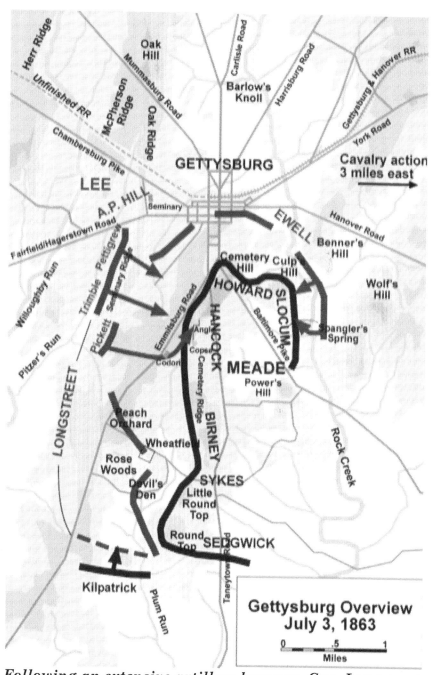

Gettysburg Overview July 3, 1863

Following an extensive artillery barrage, Gen. Longstreet reluctantly obeyed Gen. Lee's order to initiate the ill-fated attack known as Pickett's Charge. (HJ)

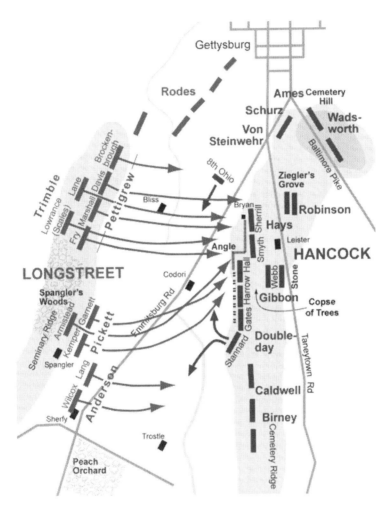

PICKETT'S CHARGE DETAIL
July 3, 1863
(HJ)

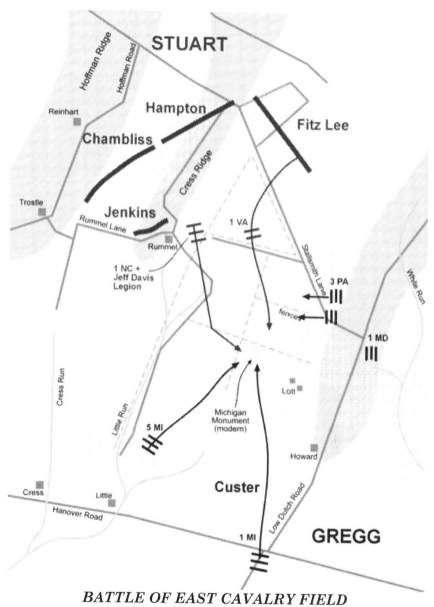

BATTLE OF EAST CAVALRY FIELD
July 3, 1863
During Pickett's Charge, Confederate Gen. J.E.B. Stuart's cavalry attacked the Union right flank, three miles east of Gettysburg. Union Gen. George Armstrong Custer led the counterattack. (HJ) Read about this crucial cavalry battle in the highly acclaimed novel, "The Unfinished Work," by Frank Meredith:
www.TheUnfinishedWork.com

Available in the following editions:
Hard cover: 336 pages, more than 50 rare maps and illustrations
Soft Cover: 320 pages (fewer maps and illustrations)
Large Print: 440 pages, text only, 16-point type, 8x10 soft cover
Kindle Edition: through the appropriate well-known website

Order autographed copies from: www.TheUnfinishedWork.com

THE UNFINISHED WORK
by Frank Meredith

June, 1863. Confederate troops invade Pennsylvania intent on winning their 2nd War of Independence, and young Jake Becker must choose: fight for southern freedom and earn the love of his Virginia belle, or defend his home and fight to end slavery? His decision puts him front and center at several pivotal events in the Gettysburg Campaign, where he discovers his ultimate call is to an even higher duty.

Like "The Killer Angels," "The Unfinished Work" features vivid, eyewitness accounts of participants on both sides of the battle lines. As in "Gone with the Wind," Eliza, a pampered southern belle, must cope with the life-changing consequences of the war, watch her lover go off to join the fight, and deal with the most unexpected rival for his affections – her sister, Kathleen.

Reviewers say . . .

"Meredith, drawing on extensive historical research, paints a vivid recreation of the Gettysburg campaign as seen by men on both sides of the battle line. The author's fictional creations are colorfully three-dimensional. Eliza, in particular, is a glorious confection of self-pity, insecurity and sugarcoated chutzpah, a downscale Scarlett O'Hara. An entertaining, human-scale rendering of the Gettysburg cataclysm." -- *Kirkus Discoveries*

"This novel is clearly written with a keen understanding of the culture of the 19th century Pennsylvania German farmers and residents, and the Civil War buff will appreciate the attention to historical detail, including some useful footnotes (unusual for a novelist to add this much appreciated touch.) For those readers who enjoy historical fiction, "The Unfinished Work" has broad appeal for both men and women, and it has an excellent storyline that holds the reader's attention." -- *Scott L. Mingus, Sr.*, Civil War historian and author

"The battles were so finely crafted that you could almost smell the smoke and feel the heat of the blasts. The budding romance between Jake and the Bigler sisters brought welcome relief to the intensity of the battles and the emotions on both sides of the war. He easily made a case for the North and the South, leaving the choice of who was right up to the individual reader." -- *News and Experts*

Made in the USA
Lexington, KY
26 October 2013